Comhairle Contae
Átha Cliath Theas
South Dublin County Council

UNCERTAINTY RULES?

Making uncertainty
work for you

We dedicate this book to our respective parents who supported and encouraged us in our early years. They have passed away but are not forgotten.

UNCERTAINTY RULES?

Making uncertainty work for you

Richard Plenty and Terri Morrissey

SERIES EDITOR: Dr Marie Murray

ATRIUM

First published in 2020 by Atrium
Atrium is an imprint of Cork University Press
Boole Library
University College Cork
Cork T12 ND89
Ireland

Library of Congress Control Number: 2019955529

Distribution in the USA Longleaf Services, Chapel Hill,
NC, USA.

British Library Cataloguing in Publication Data
A CIP catalogue record for this book is available from the
British Library.

ISBN 978-1-78205-377-4
Printed by Gutenberg in Malta
Typeset by Studio 10 Design

Cover image courtesy of pngtree.com

www.corkuniversitypress.com

CONTENTS

DR MARIE MURRAY has worked as a clinical psychologist for more than forty years across the entire developmental spectrum. An honours graduate of UCD, from where she also obtained an MSc and PhD, she is a chartered psychologist, registered family therapist and supervisor, a member of both the Irish Council for Psychotherapy and the European Association for Psychotherapy and a former member of the Heads of Psychology Services in Ireland. Key clinical posts have included being Director of Psychology in St Vincent's Psychiatric Hospital, Dublin, and Director of The Student Counselling Services in UCD. Marie served on the Medical Council of Ireland (2008–13) and on the Council of the Psychological Society of Ireland (2014–17). She has presented internationally, from the Tavistock and Portman NHS Trust in London, to Peking University, Beijing. She was an *Irish Times* columnist for eight years and has been author, co-author, contributor, and editor to a number of bestselling books, many with accompanying RTÉ radio programmes. Her appointment as Series Editor to the Cork University Press *MindYourSelf* series gathers a lifetime of professional experience to bring safe clinical information to general and professional readers.

DISCLAIMER

This book has been written for general readers to introduce the topic or to increase their knowledge and understanding of it. It is not intended, or implied, to be a substitute for professional consultation or advice in this, or allied, areas. Any content, text, graphics, images or other information provided in any of the *MindYourSelf* books is for general purposes only.

On topics that have medical, psychological, psychiatric, psychotherapy, nursing, physiotherapy, occupational therapy, educational, vocational, organisational, sociological, legal or any mental health- or physical health-related or other content, *MindYourSelf* books do not replace diagnosis, treatment, or any other appropriate professional consultations and interventions. This also applies to any information or website links contained in the book.

While every effort has been made to ensure the accuracy of the information in the book, it is possible that errors or omissions may occur. Research also leads to new multidisciplinary perspectives in all professional areas, so that, despite all the publishers' caution and care, new thinking on certain topics may alter the accuracy of the content. The authors, editors and publishers can, therefore, assume no responsibility, nor provide any guarantees or warranties concerning the up-to-date nature of the information provided.

MindYourSelf

Few expressions convey as much care as that lovely phrase 'mind yourself'. Quintessentially Irish, it is a blessing, an injunction, an endearment and a solicitous farewell. Like many simple phrases, 'mind yourself' has layers of psychological meaning, so that while it trips lightly off the tongue at the end of conversations, there are depths of kindness that accompany it.

Being told to 'mind yourself' touches the heart. It resonates with the longing in each of us to have somebody in our world who cares about us. Saying 'mind yourself' means 'you matter to me' that what happens to you is important, and may nothing bad befall you. It is a cautionary phrase, with a gentle acknowledgement of your personal responsibility in self-care. Although it has become so ingrained in our leave-taking that we may not consciously note it, unconsciously, being minded is an atavistic need in all of us. 'Mind yourself' is what parents say to children, to adolescents, what people say to each other, to family and friends. We also say it to reassure ourselves that we have reminded those we love to keep themselves safe.

It is in this spirit of recognising the importance of self-care that the *MindYourSelf* book series has been designed; to bring safe, researched, peer-reviewed information from front-line professionals to help people to mind themselves. While, at one level, information – about everything – is now on multiple platforms at the touch of a screen, relying on internet sites is a problem. What is true? Whom can you trust? How do you sift through the data to find what you need to know? Because it is not lack of access to facts, but fact overload, that makes people increasingly conscious of the dangers of misinformation, contradictory perspectives, internet prognoses, and the risk of unreliable or exploitative sources. What people want is simply the information that is relevant to them, delivered by professionals who care about their specialities and who are keen to help readers understand the topic. May this Cork University Press *MindYourSelf* series find its way to all who need it, and give readers the tools and resources to really mind themselves.

Dr Marie Murray, Series Editor, *MindYourSelf*

FOREWORD

We live in a world of change and uncertainty. The personal and collective impact of this has compromised our mental health and well-being. It has shaken our belief in institutions, weakened democracy, opened doors to despotic populism and facilitated xenophobia. Societies seem to be more anxious and less tolerant, more fearful and less flexible, and find it hard to deal with the unpredictability of life. So if ever there was a time when we need to understand the psychological influence of 'uncertainty' it is now. That is why this book, *Uncertainty Rules? Making the most of uncertainty*, is such a timely exploration of how to manage change and cope with uncertainty in ways that are practical, productive and creative.

The book proposes a systematic approach to dealing with uncertainty called the Richmor Model. Designed by the book's authors Richard Plenty and Terri Morrissey, the Richmor Model is a detailed guide on how to survive and thrive in uncertain times. It lays out a proactive, positive strategy to manage change, and discusses how to make the most of the possibilities 'uncertainty' brings. Recognising that 'uncertainty rules' – in the sense that it is a dominant force at this historical juncture – the book also explores 'rules' for coping with uncertainty. But rather than prescribing rigid rules, the book seeks to help people find their own unique solutions to the challenges they face.

By drawing an arc from the past to the present, the authors lead us into the topic. They describe the shift from what was once a seemingly secure world, to one in which the very future of the planet is in doubt. Their personal accounts of how the pace of life has altered, even in their own lifetimes, show

1

us how important it is to understand our own experiences of change. The task is to change ourselves before we try to change the world, and so Richard and Terri remind us that, 'while we may not always be able to understand or influence what is happening around us, we *do* have control over how we respond to it'.

In the various chapters of *Uncertainty Rules? Making the most of uncertainty* the authors explain the dilemmas and choices that arise from uncertainty. They emphasise the importance of time to think, the use of discretionary time throughout the various life-cycle stages, and what they call 'the fallacy of work–life balance'. They advise readers on how to think strategically, act decisively, experiment productively, develop competencies and make the most of 'uncertainty' itself.

The recommendations in the book shift from micro to macro as Richard and Terri draw on their extensive professional international experience in organisation and leadership development. They provide an eclectic mix of ideas, research, illustrations, quotations, practical examples, vignettes from history, military metaphors, motivational stories, literary references and personal inspirational narratives to support their approach. There are risks and opportunities in a world of Volatility, Uncertainty, Complexity and Ambiguity (VUCA) and, as the authors point out, the challenge is to manage the risks and seize the opportunities. There is always a balance to be kept between learning from the past, living in the present and considering the future.

Uncertainty may rule, but we must not regress – psychologically, emotionally or empathically – to primitive negativity or political polarisation as we grapple with this period of fundamental technological, geopolitical and social change.

Long before our current concerns about uncertainty, the poet John Keats coined the term 'negative capability' to describe a willingness to grasp uncertainty, live imaginatively and make peace with ambiguity. Much earlier still the philosopher Socrates made his famous paradoxical observation that the one thing he knew was that he knew nothing!

Uncertainty is not new, but in each generation, perhaps, there is a personal need to understand it, embrace it and discover how to make it work for you.

Dr Marie Murray, Series Editor, *MindYourSelf*

ACKNOWLEDGEMENTS

This is the first book we have written together. Particular mention must be made of the *MindYourSelf* Series Editor Dr Marie Murray, whose continued support and belief in this book helped bring it to fruition, and Cork University Press, especially Mike Collins, Publication Director; Maria O'Donovan, Editor; and Aonghus Meaney and Alison Burns for their help in its production.

We would also like to thank the cartoonist Simon Pearsall, whose illustrations have graced our office walls for many years (www.pearsallcartoons.com).

We must mention family members and colleagues who have supported us over the period of this venture, including Annette Plenty; Dr Amanda Clinton, Director of International Affairs of the American Psychological Association; Ed Montgomery, Managing Director of Your Healthcare; and Professor Brian Hughes, University College Galway.

We would like to acknowledge the contribution of the hundreds of participants we have taught internationally on conferences and courses, particularly in the airport sector, and our professional colleagues in universities, consultancies and client organisations. They have all helped inform, clarify and enhance our thinking.

We would also like to thank the many people who have contributed to the thinking behind this book in diverse and unexpected ways, including Ita Daly, David Wright, Ben Tompsett and Anne Plenty.

Finally, we would like to thank each other.

INTRODUCTION

'I'm really not sure that's going to work,' said Terri. 'Well if it doesn't, we'll just have to find another way,' said Richard.

The importance of uncertainty

We first became interested in uncertainty as a consequence of consulting and teaching change management for many years. The more we worked with change programmes, the more we realised that they rarely worked out as planned. At that time traditional change models were based on simply establishing the gap between a 'vision' and the 'current reality' and systematically planning how to close it.

We found that, in practice, this approach was rarely sufficient. Circumstances changed and the unexpected happened. We learned to appreciate the wisdom demonstrated many years before by Oscar Wilde, who had pronounced that: 'To expect the unexpected shows a thoroughly modern intellect.'

As our society has become more complex, the level of uncertainty has increased, and the general population has been affected. Increasingly people find they must learn to deal with evolving situations which do not fit their previous experience and where the outcome is uncertain. The pace of change has become much faster, with technology and social media creating a 24/7 'always on' culture and a demand for a more immediate response and expectation for instantaneous feedback.

We have noticed that people cope in different ways, for example:

• Many people look for immediate solutions. Finding that uncertainty makes them anxious, they will do almost anything to avoid it. Their focus is on taking steps to reduce their own anxiety rather than seeking to understand the situation and coming up with a rational response. Typically, this involves either reverting to what they are familiar with or following someone who claims to have the 'right' answer.

• Others get stuck. Finding it hard to accept that they are not in control, they prefer to keep risks to an absolute minimum. They become obsessed with ever-deeper analysis and find it difficult to make choices and to be decisive. This is a pattern that can affect successful people who become overly concerned about the possibility of failure.

• A few people seem to be flexible, adaptable and adventurous enough to enjoy uncertainty and make the most of the opportunities that it provides. They seek to understand the overall situation and suspend judgement until they have sufficient information. They exhibit an appetite for risk but in a calculated way. They tend to be quick to spot opportunities, are not put off by risk, do not seem to be particularly stressed, and maintain good relationships with a wide variety of people. They are action-oriented and prepared to try things out, relying on a combination of intuition and facts to make decisions.

Our experience is that many people do not deal with uncertainty very well. Our belief is that if we do not learn how to cope better with it, we run the risk of creating societies that could return us to the Dark Ages. During such periods, rather than seeking the truth, people seek certainty. Some signs are already evident with the rapid growth of populism and populist movements internationally.

Those who do not manage uncertainty adopt stereotyped views and are convinced they are right and others wrong. They do not listen to those who are different from them and consequently they may fail to develop understanding, empathy or sensitivity to different perspectives. They are not open to challenge. This encourages a 'head in the sand' mentality, which does not lead to optimal results.

This is a slippery path. History shows us that if we go down this road, there is a risk of coercion, abuse of power and ultimately fascism. As Anatole France said, 'It is the certainty that they possess the truth that makes men cruel.'

On the other hand, if we can raise people's ability to manage uncertainty, there could be tangible opportunities for us to find new and better solutions to complex problems. With the information that is available to us, as well as the level of education and connectivity we now have, we should be able to think through, address and resolve many of these issues by coming up with innovative solutions that can be deployed widely and rapidly, as well as developing our own capabilities along the way.

Why we have written this book

We have written this book as part of the *MindYourSelf* series to describe the individual and personal skills and approaches which we have found work best in uncertain times so that people will understand how to cope better with uncertainty and manage change more effectively. Our aim is to help increase the number of people who feel capable and competent working in complex and uncertain environments. We have come up with a straightforward approach which we have called the Richmor Model, which we think is useful. As a way of thinking about uncertainty, we use the metaphor of navigating our way through a mountain range where conditions are unpredictable and changing.

This book brings together our personal experiences as well as incorporating research, knowledge and examples from a wide variety of sources. We have told stories from our own lives to try to make the concepts we describe come alive and to illustrate better what we mean. We have also drawn extensively on what we have learned over the years from working with senior leaders in large organisations on complex, strategic change. Many of these people found that their roles were as much about the best way to deal with uncertainty as delivering planned change. They are at the sharp end of uncertainty, so there is much to learn from them.

We have endeavoured to ensure that the foundations of our thinking are well referenced, and that our proposed approach is clearly enough articulated to facilitate testing against empirical data. We have chosen the title 'Uncertainty Rules' deliberately: our 'rules' reflect a set of loosely held principles which are open to challenge and debate. They won't apply to every situation, but should help in most.

Dealing with uncertainty is a major human challenge, requiring a combination of intuition, logic, resilience and self-awareness. To do it well requires the ability to think critically, to work at it, and to have the courage to try things out. Many of the ideas we describe are similar to those taught on leadership programmes, but they won't have been put together in this way before and certainly are not yet widely used in everyday life in the ways that we present and explain.

What are the qualities that matter?

Qualities that we have found to be important in making the most of uncertainty include:

• Having the courage to think independently. Intellectually, we need to get into the habit of looking objectively at the big picture and not be afraid to 'reframe' and change our opinions as new information emerges. A sense of perspective is critical – and a sense of humour helps.

• Accepting responsibility for ourselves rather than blaming others. Developing a clear idea of 'who we are' and 'who we want to be' provides a purpose and context which makes things a lot easier.

• Being proactive. A readiness to take the initiative is critical. Building confidence is important; curiosity helps; self-discipline matters; resilience and perseverance are essential.

• Being prepared to take a risk. Trying things out and learning from failures as well as successes is key, accepting that things may not always go right the first time.

• The ability to collaborate with, listen to and influence others is important. Respecting others with a different background and point of view is a value which is critical but sometimes appears to have 'gone missing' in a polarised world.

At first glance, it may look like this list of characteristics represents an unlikely combination of qualities for any one individual to possess, present perhaps in exceptional individuals but not in most of us. Yet these qualities are exactly those which we address in this book, because their development is possible and the rewards of doing so are great.

Who is this book for?

We have written this book with a broad target audience in mind, including those who pick it up in a bookshop, curious about the topic and what it might mean for them personally; for those in leadership roles who are thinking about the impact of uncertainty on their teams, organisations, businesses or services; for academics, consultants, coaches and trainers who are interested in this field or perhaps already involved in it.

This is how we think the book will work for you:

For the general reader. At a personal level, all of us must find ways of dealing with uncertainty in our lives. This means finding ways of taking back control, realising that while we may not always be able to understand or influence what is happening around us, we do have control over how we choose to respond to it.

For those in leadership roles. The skills we describe in this book are relevant for leaders at all levels, not just those at the very top. Robust approaches to dealing with uncertainty involve building organisation capability and capacity at the front line, empowering and energising local services and teams to find their own solutions within an overall strategy rather than imposing solutions from the top down.

For academics, consultants, coaches and trainers. We hope the book provides useful material and a conceptual framework for teaching and coaching. We have developed our approach based on a combination of our personal experiences as individuals, leaders, consultants, psychologists and teachers and an eclectic combination of academic, literary and popular influences and sources.

How is this book structured?

The topic of the book is attended to in the various chapters in the following way. In Chapters 1–3, we look at the context of uncertainty and discuss how our world is changing and the issues and dilemmas this poses for us. We also describe logical and psychological strategies for dealing with uncertainty. In Chapters 4–8, we look systematically at the best way to approach uncertain situations, drawing on a combination of theory and our own experience to describe an overall approach, the Richmor Model, that we believe is well suited to this kind of environment. This overall approach is described in Chapter 4. Chapters 5–8 then describe each of the four steps in more detail. In the final chapters of the book Chapters 9–11 we address the issue of mastering uncertainty as we look at how these ideas can be applied in practice. We examine the skills required to 'mind ourselves' in an uncertain world and consider what attitudes and behaviours make the most sense and why. In the final chapter we look at the broader implications for organisations and society.

CHAPTER 1

An Uncertain World

'This book is based on many hours of heated discussion and argument,' said Terri. 'No it isn't,' said Richard.

Life used to be so simple …

We grew up in different countries, Ireland and Britain, in very different circumstances: Terri the daughter of a career Irish civil servant and Richard the son of a building and construction manager who had been a Spitfire fighter pilot in the Second World War.

The character of the two countries was quite different during our childhood years: Ireland was still in the grip of a strong authoritarian and moralistic Roman Catholic Church while England was in a postwar 'never had it so good' phase with the libertarian 'swinging sixties' in full swing. In Britain divorce was still rare; in Ireland it was illegal. In Britain most people stayed in the same area for life, but in Ireland emigration had been a feature of life for many years.

Despite these differences, there was a great deal of similarity in our day-to-day lives. Both our fathers had risen to middle-class jobs from poor backgrounds. Our lives were relatively straightforward and typical of our contemporaries. Our mothers looked after us at home, and our fathers went to work, leaving and returning at the same time each day and doing the same job in the same office for many years. Richard's parents later ran a dancing school in the evenings, but only after their children had left home.

We both had access to one black-and-white TV channel (BBC) and watched the same children's TV programmes at the same time of day (it was some time before RTÉ started to broadcast in Ireland). Food for both of us was always meat or fish, potatoes and vegetables, the menu depending largely on the day of the week.

Societal expectations were that you went to school and did as well as you could in your studies. If you were very clever, you went to university. The aim for most was to get a secure job, ideally one for life, with a safe employer, get married, buy a house and have a family. Women then left their jobs to become housewives, while men were expected to keep working until retirement.

In retrospect, the middle to late twentieth century represents the high point of a period when scientific and technological 'certainty' had been on the rise for hundreds of years. What was mystical or magical had become intelligible: for example, the discovery of the laws of gravitation made the prediction of solar eclipses routine whereas in earlier times these were seen as frightening portents of doom. Innovations in technology literally made the world easier to navigate: the discovery of practical ways of measuring longitude not only made international travel easier, but led to a shared system for measuring time, allowing clocks in different places to be synchronised.

Advances in understanding had ushered in an era of education and enlightenment. Mass education, books, radio, TV and films increased people's knowledge and understanding of the world. Common production methods, services and products were making many aspects of urban and suburban lives more similar internationally. The same kinds of jobs, careers and lifestyles were emerging in cities around the world.

Indeed, life itself became more predictable than it had ever been. Medicine was becoming increasingly effective. While the detailed statistics are subject to challenge and debate given the different ways data has been collected over the years and the difficulties of proving causation, the overall evidence indicates that improved health systems increased life expectancy. They did so, for example, by reducing infant mortality and the chance of dying randomly through an incurable disease. Life expectancy at birth in seventeenth-century England was about thirty-five years, by 1900 it was closer to fifty and by the 1950s it was around sixty-five. It is currently around eighty years, with many people living into their nineties and beyond.

At the same time, societies became more civilised and, despite people feeling under threat because of the speed at which information reaches us about negative events, there is now less risk of being killed through random violence than ever before. The available data suggests that the chances of being murdered in Europe have reduced by around fifty times since the Middle Ages.

Although these advances have been positive, the social changes that accompanied them have not always been easy for people to adjust to. For example, the pace of scientific and technological progress caused considerable social and psychological disruption in the nineteenth century in Victorian England, where people, bewildered by the ferocious pace of change, did what they could to maintain appearances of stability and respectability.

By the middle to late twentieth century, however, these insecurities were less evident. The British Prime Minister Harold Macmillan famously told the British people in 1957 that they had never had it so good. A more stable world seemed to have arrived. Ireland, too, appeared to be settling into independence as a republic and trying to fashion a way of life that would be more secure than in previous times.

These certainties were reflected in the way our education systems were developed and institutionalised. Acquiring knowledge and understanding was something you did when you were young – and what you learned was expected to last a lifetime. Schedules, including lesson times and breaks, were fixed and predetermined. In schools the focus was on individual acquisition of information through formal lessons, delivered by teachers who transmitted their knowledge via blackboard and chalk to the notebooks of their pupils. A few standard textbooks provided the basis of the curriculum. Rigorous written examinations tested the ability of the students to remember and regurgitate the information they had been given. Regardless of methodology, there was an appreciation of education, and an understanding that its provision to as many as possible was beneficial for society

On leaving the education system, the jobs people took up were also usually well structured and organised. Generally organisations were bureaucratic and hierarchical, with a very clear chain of command. Many specialist jobs, trades and professions continued as they had done for years. Those who worked in factories or production roles often had simple, clear, regular, repetitive roles. There were many clerical, middle management and administrative positions, which for the most part existed in highly stable organisations. People stayed in the same job for years. We have heard (admittedly unconfirmed) stories about one organisation in Germany where not only the job titles but also the names of the job holders were carved in concrete above the office entrance. Even if not actually true, it serves as a metaphor for the stability of an era that has long since disappeared.

So when people say 'life used to be so simple', they are referring to a time when choices were more limited and the outcomes more predictable than they are today. Between then and now the world has changed dramatically: there has been a technological and internet revolution, and societal values have been transformed.

Very few young people today could confidently predict the pattern of their future lives in the way their parents and grandparents could.

A world of increasing complexity

So why has the process of 'increasing certainty' gone into reverse for the first time in many years?

The prime reason is that advances in automation, technology and the internet have been taking place at a rate that has proved impossible to anticipate. Whole industries have disappeared as technology has overtaken them and new ones have taken their place. At the same time, costs have plummeted, allowing more and more people access to information technology, communication platforms and opportunities to travel.

There is a far greater level of consumer and personal choice than ever before. There are literally hundreds of thousands of TV and radio channels available to us all, for example, while the variety of food and drink at our disposal has increased dramatically.

Thanks to the internet, we are increasingly part of a global community, with opportunities to connect with others of a similar perspective, wherever they are in the world. It has allowed us to keep in touch with distant friends and colleagues – as well as providing a platform for political populism.

This connectivity also makes an enormous difference at the broader systems level. What happens in the technology domain (e.g. automation) could have a profound effect on social values (e.g. through concerns about the impact on jobs), which could cause an immediate populist reaction (e.g. protectionism), which might impact on personal choice (e.g. freedom to travel) and be amplified very quickly (through social media) with unpredictable political consequences. Or it might not.

Indeed, as technology and technological solutions are deployed on a much larger scale and at a faster rate than in the past, the 'side effects' are becoming more obvious. Environmental costs are substantial and pose a threat to our planet as a whole through the greenhouse effect and global warming. There is a social cost to rapid change – even when this results ultimately in higher living standards – as existing jobs are lost and communities face a threat to their survival. Geopolitical power is in a phase of transition as countries such as China and India become globally significant economies. This translates into enormous challenges for our political systems.

This political challenge is all the greater because the impact of technological progress on social values has been unexpected and pervasive, and remains a 'work in progress'. Who could have imagined the legislative changes in Ireland with regard to same-sex marriage and abortion? Who could have imagined the extent to which Irish society now embraces diversity and an enormous variety of lifestyles as commonplace? And who could have imagined all this in a world where people live on average more than twenty years longer than they used to?

Disruption has become the new norm. Events, external shocks and surprises that are sometimes impossible to predict, particularly in the political arena, have the potential to become greatly magnified once a system becomes connected. News travels fast with social media and relatively small events can go 'viral', spreading ideas and concerns whether they be true or false.

All this has been encapsulated in the phrase 'a VUCA world'. This is a world model of Volatility, Uncertainty, Complexity and Ambiguity which has been used extensively in large organisations and the military as a basis for developing and testing strategy.

• **V**olatility refers to the rate at which situations and circumstances can change from one state to another in unpredictable ways.

• **U**ncertainty is the subject of this book.

• **C**omplexity means that there are less likely to be simple relationships between cause and effect in systems which are highly connected.

• **A**mbiguity alludes to the increased difficulty in providing one simple explanation which everyone accepts using the same set of data. There are always different perspectives and interpretations of the same problem. It has never been harder to say definitively whether the glass is half empty or half full.

In a VUCA world we can no longer predict the future with any certainty. The world has changed, and we need to adjust and adapt to these new realities. How can we learn to manage the risks associated with this and at the same time seize the associated opportunities?

These opportunities arise because of the variability inherent in uncertainty. The liberating impact of uncertainty should never be underestimated. Uncertain times provide the greatest opportunity for change, innovation and creativity. Custom and habit can be very difficult to free ourselves from, and the disruptive effects of uncertainty give us a chance to break the mould and try out new ideas. Operational businesses may prefer environments where they can plan with a little more confidence, but entrepreneurs can welcome the possibilities that uncertainty brings.

It is not only entrepreneurs who can benefit, however. There are great opportunities associated with a VUCA world for society as a whole. Political and social freedom and change are often associated with periods of uncertainty. This is also when so many possibilities for technological and social innovation present themselves, as well as artistic and literary creativity. These are the times when it can be most exciting to be alive.

The psychological impact

Despite the opportunities that uncertainty can bring, our experience has been that the first reaction of most people to the word 'uncertainty' is negative. This is hardly surprising, as uncertainty can provoke considerable anxiety.

Indeed, some research on the 'social brain' suggests that uncertain situations can feel highly threatening, because they can activate the brain's 'primary threat' circuitry and associated networks. From this perspective, an extreme perceived threat to our sense of certainty can activate similar brain networks as a threat to our life, particularly if we see the situation as unfair or if there is a possibility that our status or autonomy are at risk.

Whatever the physiological mechanisms at play, there can be a tendency for us to react emotionally rather than rationally to uncertainty, particularly if we feel that we are isolated and do not have the 'psychological safety' of support from people we consider to be friends. We may become aggressive and disruptive; we may become very anxious, thinking of all the things that could go wrong; or we may just try and 'block things out', finding ways of ignoring reality. We may even panic.

The ambiguity inherent in complex situations means that different interpretations are always possible. If we are anxious about uncertainty, or just impatient, then one way of dealing with this is to oversimplify. This may not be an issue if it helps us cope, but it doesn't necessarily lead to optimum solutions. As serious polarisation of world views and stereotyping of those who are different appears to be a growing problem, amplified by social media, what is alarming is the lack of dialogue, communication or understanding that sometimes emerges.

Prolonged periods of volatility can have a paralysing effect. The speed of change means that it can be difficult to know whether that change will endure. Change fatigue sets in and people cease to buy-in or adjust, particularly when they feel that the new order is being imposed on them for not especially good reasons.

Our experience is that if we insist on things always being stable and organised, if we demand to know exactly what we are supposed to do and what everything means before agreeing to act – and if we become obsessed with following 'custom and practice' and tradition – then we are less likely to be effective in situations of uncertainty, and can block others from adopting a more sensible, pragmatic approach. *The Hitchhiker's Guide to the Galaxy* contains the memorable phrase 'We demand rigidly defined areas of doubt and uncertainty', which captures perfectly the essence of this mindset.

There is a cultural element at play here. The Dutch social psychologist Gerard (Geert) Hofstede has described how different nationalities have different degrees of tolerance to uncertain or ambiguous situations. Countries with relatively low 'uncertainty avoidance' (e.g. Ireland, the UK, the USA, China and India) are generally prepared to accept a less structured approach, with the capacity to flex and adapt their rules to different circumstances and pragmatically 'muddle through' solutions. Countries with high 'uncertainty avoidance' (e.g. France, Italy, Russia and South Korea) prefer to have clear procedures and rules in place to cater for all possible eventualities.

Uncertainty is tolerated much better once we learn to accept that there may not be simple solutions to problems. Uncertain situations are characterised by ambiguity and doubt, and there is a need to accept that it is not always possible to spell out all the details in advance. Being prepared to learn as you go along is more appropriate. Seeing problems as an ongoing series of dilemmas to be addressed, where some 'muddling through' is necessary, is important.

There are also those who genuinely enjoy uncertainty. Personality is a factor. Some people are inherently more adventurous than others, welcoming the excitement of potential change and the opportunities that can go with it, rather than being wary of potential risks. Those who are open to learning, who are curious, outward-looking, resilient and emotionally stable, are likely to have a higher tolerance to uncertainty than others.

Education makes a difference. Our observation has been that those who are well educated and are used to having to think things through for themselves are often more comfortable dealing with complexity and managing uncertainty than those who have had less opportunity to do so. They may be less prone to stereotyping and accepting simplistic solutions. Of course, this is no guarantee that, in the final analysis, their views will always turn out to be right.

Can we learn to deal better with uncertainty?

So the challenge that we face as individuals, organisations and societies is how best to manage ourselves in the context of a world which is likely to be in geopolitical, technological and societal transition, and more volatile, complex and uncertain than ever before.

Will we be able to cope with the ambiguities associated with this? Will we be able to manage our anxieties? Can we find a way of dealing with the conflicts that arise? Will we be able to take advantage of opportunities?

One reason for optimism is that we may well be getting better at it already. The average intelligence of the population has been increasing by around 3 IQ points per decade, the so-called Flynn effect, which is an enormous shift that should lead to our societal capacity to deal with uncertainty increasing over time. This IQ increase may be due to our increased exposure to complexity from an early age.

DOES EARLY EXPOSURE TO COMPLEXITY INCREASE IQ?
(Richard)

The increasing richness of our environment is often cited as an explanation for the general rise in IQ which has taken place over recent years. Consider, for example, the popular BBC children's television series aimed at one- to six-year olds, 'In the Night Garden'. A group of many diverse characters – including Igglepiggle, Makka Pakka, Upsy Daisy, the Tombliboos, the Pontipines, the Wottingers, the Haahoos, the Ninky Nonk and the Pinky Ponk – take part in live-action scenarios involving a variety of activities and interactions. Contrast that with the first children's TV shows broadcast by the BBC in the mid-twentieth century, for example 'Bill and Ben the Flowerpot Men'. In this series, there were just three 'static' characters – Bill and Ben (who lived in flowerpots) and a (female) 'Weed' – in between them. Conversations and plots were simple. The increase in complexity since then is remarkable.

While the very young may be learning to cope with complexity, what about the rest of us? Is there still hope? Our starting point must be to recognise that the kind of world many of us used to live in, where for a relatively brief historical period most people and organisations experienced relatively long periods of stability and predictability, has disappeared for now. It may return, though in a different format. In the meantime we need to adjust and adapt the ways we act and behave if we are to keep pace with the current reality.

Our education, training and social conditioning has equipped us to deal with a relatively simple world, one that was fairly predictable and where there were accepted rules and guidelines in place. In such a world we were able to operate in accordance with agreed custom and practice rather than having to think too deeply about issues. While many of the circumstances we encounter in everyday life remain the same, the balance has changed, and we face increasingly complex, changing and novel situations.

To deal successfully with uncertain, fluid and demanding challenges requires a different mindset and attitude, as well as learning new behaviours and skills. In uncertain times, we don't have maps we can rely on. Instead we have to think much more for ourselves, challenging our assumptions and coming up with creative ideas. We need to take personal responsibilty for working things out in the particular circumstances in which we find ourselves, and have the courage to do things differently, where necessary. And we have to do this in an environment where nothing is likely to be 'black and white' or clear-cut.

CHAPTER 2
Dilemmas and Choices

'There's always two sides to every coin,' said Richard.
'But how can they ever be separated?' replied Terri.

The dilemmas we face ...

I n the book and BBC radio series *The Hitchhiker's Guide to the Galaxy*, the hero Arthur Dent – a quiet, unassuming man from a village in south-western England – is faced with a succession of bizarre, unpredictable events and circumstances to which he has to respond. He carries with him a guidebook, 'The Hitchhiker's Guide', which contains detailed information on how to behave in all sorts of scenarios. Recognising, though, that in a crisis it may not always be possible to read the instructions from the manual in detail, the book has just one summary instruction written in large letters on the front – 'DON'T PANIC!'

In an emergency, it is always a good idea to keep our cool. It is not the time to stop thinking. Unfortunately, the choices we have to make when responding to uncertainty are not usually as straightforward as this. Most of the time we must decide how best to respond to longer-term evolving situations where there are no immediate threats and where the consequences of our approach only become apparent over time. These are tricky things to balance.

We might prefer clarity, but in practice we are often faced with a continual series of dilemmas which need to be addressed if we are to determine the best approach to take. The solutions will rarely be black or white; there are likely to be difficult choices to make. Here are some of the dilemmas that are most common in an uncertain environment.

Action or patience?

How to make decisions that stand the test of time in an unpredictable, uncertain environment is a key practical challenge. There is generally a balance to be struck between being decisive and being patient:

• Being decisive and making a quick decision. This reduces complexity by minimising the number of variables to be managed, but it can be risky if decisions are made before all the facts have come to light. On the other hand, decisive action allows us to shape the 'field of play' and may give us a competitive edge.

• Being patient and postponing decisions until the situation becomes clearer. Provided we can manage our own emotions and others' anxiety, this keeps our options open and gives us more flexibility and room to manoeuvre as circumstances evolve. It may prove to be the wiser course. On the other hand, we could miss opportunities by being too slow and over-cautious.

Let us take a simple example. Imagine we are out shopping. We suddenly realise we have invited a friend for lunch that day but can't remember exactly what arrangements were agreed. She is not answering her phone as she is in a meeting, so we buy some food at the supermarket anyway while we can. It seems like a good idea and means we don't have to worry about not having something to eat. We don't want to be embarrassed.

But once we have done that, we have reduced our options. What if our lunch guest turns out to be a vegetarian and does not like the meat we bought? What if we eventually remember that we had actually planned to meet at a restaurant? Would it have been more sensible to have postponed our decision to buy the food until we had a chance to contact our friend and check the arrangements we had made?

In this trivial example, it would not matter in practice whether we had thought things through in any depth. But if we aspire to get things right consistently, we need to get into the habit of thinking more deeply. By doing so we are less likely to be caught off-guard in situations where the stakes are higher – and where it would be unwise to make impulsive decisions just because we want to reduce uncertainty and minimise our own anxiety.

'Deciding on decisiveness' is complicated because the relationship between cause and effect is less clear in 'uncertain' situations than in 'certain' ones. It can be hard to know if what we are doing now is really likely to get the outcomes we desire. The past is not necessarily a reliable guide to the future. For example, applications to British universities are declining for the first time in years as people wonder whether it is worth paying high fees for third-level education in a world where the historical link between job prospects, salary and education may not continue.

A pragmatic response, taking one step at a time, is generally sensible in very uncertain situations, particularly when the stakes are high. Keeping options open is helpful as long as it does not lead to people becoming paralysed by fear or anxiety and ultimately 'missing the boat'.

Boldness can have its own rewards, but common sense and pragmatism matter too.

Planning or improvisation?

Because uncertainty breaks the straightforward link between experience and future outcomes, detailed planning becomes very difficult.

In 'certain' situations, people know what to expect, and they develop mental models which enable them to plan. For example, if you know from many previous journeys that it generally takes forty-five minutes to commute to work by train, you can work out when you need to leave home to get to work on time. If you know the train timetables and the current time, you can predict quite accurately when you will arrive.

This becomes much more difficult to do in 'uncertain' situations, when circumstances may change unexpectedly. If trains are delayed because of adverse weather conditions, it is more difficult to estimate how long the journey will take. If there is even more uncertainty, for example a threat of last-minute industrial action by train drivers, it may be that the trains will not even run. Predicting a time of arrival with any degree of confidence in these circumstances becomes even harder.

Faced with this situation, the usual detailed planning and routine around the daily train journey is less useful. Indeed, the most punctual person may be the only one who on the spur of the moment manages to persuade someone to give them a lift in their car. Improvising can often be as useful as trying to plan everything in advance.

In uncertain situations, it is usually best to plan in a general way rather than in detail, looking at different options but not trying to spell everything out in advance. It's also an opportunity to consider innovative solutions. In our train example, this might mean assessing the options for working from home.

Past, present or future?

The examples above illustrate how the concept of uncertainty is intimately bound up with the way we look at time – in essence, how confident we are about predicting the future. From a broader perspective, then, it's important that we balance appropriately learning from the past, living in the present and considering the future.

Past: When we adopt a 'past' orientation, we focus on looking at things from an historical perspective. We take the view that if we don't learn from history, we are destined to repeat it.

• Have we come across this kind of thing before?

• What can we learn from those who have already been through similar experiences?

The focus is on learning from the past, respecting and considering what has happened before. The emphasis is usually on tradition and continuity, but evidence-based approaches and best practice learning also have a past orientation because they look at what has already happened, albeit in a very systematic manner.

Looking at history is important and can provide some reassurance by focusing on what has already worked. At the same time, it is rarely sufficient in dealing with uncertainty, as the future may turn out to be quite different from the past, in which case previous experience is unlikely to be always a good guide to the best course of action.

THE MAGINOT LINE

The Maginot Line, named after the French minister of war André Maginot, was a line of concrete fortifications, obstacles, and weapon installations built by France in the 1930s to deter invasion by Germany. It dominated French military thinking in the inter-war years.

France had suffered appalling damage to both people and buildings in the First World War and decided to adopt a military strategy that would simply stop any form of German invasion again. The Maginot Line was designed to physically block tanks and armoured vehicles and was impervious to most forms of attack. It was such an impressive piece of construction that dignitaries from around the world visited it.

It became a military liability, however, when the Germans attacked France in the spring of 1940. Instead of attacking directly, the Germans invaded through the Low Countries, bypassing the line to the north, a tactic that completely emasculated the Maginot Line's purpose.

The Maginot Line strategy was too simple and had not kept pace with advances in military technology and thinking. The line has since become a metaphor for expensive efforts that offer a false sense of security.

Present: When we adopt a 'present' orientation, our focus is on the 'here and now' and the activities of the moment. We do not worry too much about what may or may not happen in the future – or how we might shape it.

We adopt a 'just get on with it' mentality. Control is exercised through an intense focus on ourselves and our own behaviour and emotions. Our focus is on being fully 'present', on relationships, living in the moment and going with the flow, paying attention to being fully aware and responding to changing circumstances as they arise. We pay attention to what is happening at the present time and respond to the 'here and now'.

It is perhaps not surprising that a 'present' orientation is the default for situations which are dependent on fate or chance. If you are powerless to change your environment, it makes sense to focus on what you can influence – that is, yourself.

Recently, this approach has become rather fashionable. We have become conscious of the usefulness of meditation and the importance of being aware of, and master of, our inner selves. The explosion of interest in mindfulness, where we learn to observe our feelings, thoughts and emotions without judgement, is testament to that.

What are the issues in relying solely on a 'present' perspective? Well, if we only focus on the present, this could imply a sense of helplessness in the face of external forces outside our control, which is not really the case. There are few situations in practice which are impossible to influence. Living too much in the present may encourage us to feel more like a cork bobbing up and down in a rough sea than a surfer confidently riding the crest of a wave.

A preoccupation with the 'here and now' can also mean that insufficient attention is paid to learning from experience or planning ahead. Opportunities may be missed, and things left too late. If you don't 'bite the bullet' and invest when you are young, how can you expect a pension when you are older?

Future: There are times when our responses may be more future oriented, when we are more interested in where we are headed than in our current circumstances or what happened in the past. We focus on prospects, potential, possibilities and future achievements rather than the more mundane current reality.

The simplest way of adopting a future orientation is to envisage an ideal future and then reason backwards to work out the steps we need to take to get there. We create the illusion of certainty by having a clear goal and a structured process for making it happen.

This works well when there is a clear, motivating and widely shared aspiration. Objectives that resonate with people and tap into their feelings can provide a powerful emotional engine, for example 'to win more Olympic medals', 'to put a man on the moon by the end of the decade', 'to take back control', 'to make America great again'.

This simple approach does not always work. Circumstances can change and make the original aspirations seem increasingly impractical or less relevant. The problem then is that there is so much emotional and personal investment tied up in the initial vision that people are reluctant to abandon it, even in the face of changing evidence. Aspiration can turn to inflexibility.

A more sophisticated approach is to try and imagine a number of possible scenarios leading to different outcomes. We can use these scenarios to test the viability and robustness of whatever vision we have come up with.

Intuition or logic?

Intuition, the ability to understand something instinctively without the need for conscious reasoning, comes naturally to us. We tend to navigate our everyday lives based on intuition and gut feeling rather than cool, hard logic. We are more like Captain Kirk in *Star Trek* than the logical Vulcan, Mr Spock.

Being able to act decisively and quickly has given our species an evolutionary advantage in a world where survival has, up to now, depended as much on speed of response as developing an in-depth understanding of what is happening.

Intuition is an essential tool in dealing with uncertainty, where the issues aren't always black and white, the options aren't generally obvious and even the data may not be clear. This is because our intuitive brains are brilliant at bringing together and integrating our experience based on a range of sometimes subtle cues.

To understand the limitations of intuition, however, we need to understand how it develops. Each of us sees the world from our own perspective and builds our own mental models through life experience to help us simplify the world and aid our decision-making. Our brains integrate sensory perceptions, emotional responses and data in line with our models, and in ways we are not consciously aware of, to help us navigate our way. Lessons from outside experience – dialogue and discussion with others as well as art, science, literature, music, film and drama – help to shape our mental models and ensure that they are as up-to-date and comprehensive as possible.

Unfortunately, intuition can be flawed because of the assumptions and biases that are part of our mental models. Over the last few years there has been a wealth of research by psychologists – including Daniel Kahneman, the Nobel-Prize-winning Israeli-American psychologist and economist, and his collaborator, the late Amos Tversky, renowned for his work in cognitive science on decision-making – showing that, quite apart from any individual flaws in our models, there are a number of common biases that people share which can lead to incorrect conclusions.

Those biases that are particularly relevant in times of uncertainty include:

• Self-confidence: we believe that our judgement and abilities are better than they are.

• Optimism: we tend to underestimate the downside risk of our chosen course of action and be over-optimistic about the benefits.

• Confirmation bias: we look for data to support our preconceived ideas rather than looking at the evidence with an open mind.

• Sunk costs bias: we favour something because we have already invested in it rather than rationally evaluating it on the basis of what is needed going forward.

• Loss aversion: we give undue weight to preserving what we have.

For these reasons, it is rarely sensible to rely entirely on intuition and gut feeling when navigating uncertain or complex situations. It is important to check the facts, solicit different opinions, welcome challenges and make sure we consider as many different perspectives, possibilities and outcomes as possible. It is also a good discipline to be aware of the assumptions that are being made.

Taking notice of our intuition in uncertain times is essential. Relying on it totally is rash.

CENTRAL BANK PSYCHOLOGY: ENSURING INTUITION IS KEPT IN CHECK

Andrew Haldane, chief economist at the Bank of England, spoke in 2014 about the psychological biases that can affect policy-making in central banks. The failure to predict the financial crisis of 2007 and 2008 had caused the Bank of England to rethink its approach to developing strategy. They identified 'groupthink' (members of working groups and teams going along with the views of others even when they disagree) as a principal concern and added in some additional biases – 'preference', 'myopia' and 'hubris' – that they felt were relevant to the public policy domain. They defined 'preference' as the decision-maker putting personal objectives ahead of societal ones; 'myopia' as the condition in which immediate gratification is given more weight than long-term outcomes and 'hubris' related to over-confident individuals who are more likely to be promoted to influential positions and then set unrealistic targets.

This thinking has led to a redesign of institutional frameworks for policy development. The bank does not set its own objectives, has a number of independent policy committees, and deliberately commissions research which is not based on the prevailing assumptions.

Persistence or changing course?

Persistence makes it more likely that we will achieve results. People who demonstrate persistence are not put off by the inevitable obstacles they encounter in implementing a course of action in challenging situations. As circumstances change, they are prepared to adjust and adapt their behaviour in order to reach their ultimate objective.

At the same time, blind perseverance is risky in uncertain times. What if our course of action turns out to be misguided, for reasons that we weren't able to anticipate? The problem is that even if we find ourselves continually having to readjust and adapt in order to achieve an increasingly unattainable objective, it can be almost impossible to change course. The more investment that we make in something, the less inclined we are to give up, even if the facts suggest we should (the 'sunk costs' bias). Not only do we not want to waste what we have already done, we don't like to lose face and admit we may have got things wrong.

These difficulties are compounded because it's rarely clear when it's time to change course. Giving up too quickly can be counterproductive anyway. More often than not, we know that we are bound to live through prolonged periods of uncertainty if we are to achieve challenging goals. We have learned not to give up just because we feel stressed, frustrated or disillusioned from time to time: we know this is part of the struggle we all need to go through if we are to achieve our dreams.

Still, if we find that we are failing to meet our initial expectations, it makes sense to pause and take stock, especially if we feel that our tactics aren't working as we had planned. It is also sensible to review things if it becomes clear that an alternative course of action may be far more promising, though we need to beware of developing a 'grass is always greener' mentality. And we should always re-evaluate our approach if there has been a major change in circumstances since we set our original objectives.

Stick or twist? There can be a very fine line between persistence and stupidity.

CHAPTER 3
Logic and Psychologic

'I'd rather deal with difficult situations rationally and logically,'
said Richard. 'What if it's all a mess? Then you need a heart
as well as a head!' replied Terri.

Logical approaches

L et us start with the practical. What is the best way to go about things when we are unsure about what might happen in practice? How can we 'make things happen' in an environment of uncertainty? What is the best way to make decisions?

To answer these questions, and to understand how systems at different levels of complexity behave, it's helpful to borrow from systems theory and the 'Cynefin Framework', developed by Dave Snowden when he worked for IBM Global Services.

Consider four archetypal systems: simple, complicated, complex and chaotic. We have represented this in the schematic diagram below. At one end of the scale, simple

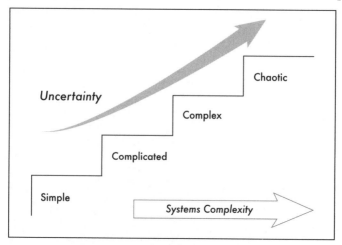

systems show a direct relationship between cause and effect; at the other, chaotic systems show no connection. Complicated and complex systems lie in between. More uncertainty is associated with higher levels of complexity.

Simple systems are at the 'certain' end of the spectrum. In simple systems, if rules are obeyed and procedures followed, results will come. For example, all you have to do with a 'ready to cook' meal is put it in the microwave, follow the instructions and the meal will emerge steaming hot and ready to eat. It's predictable and repeatable.

When people say things are 'well organised', they usually mean that the system is simple. Once a tricky problem has been thoroughly researched, understood and analysed, it may be possible to codify it. Only limited expertise is necessary to get things to work; there is no need for people to think too deeply. This is the way that organisations, bureaucracies, mass production and mass transit have developed. It is a world where standardised procedures and checklists are the order of the day. Checklists are often associated with simple systems and can be effective aide-memoires – but they have their limitations when circumstances don't fit the expected pattern.

The risk with simple systems is that if the rules continue to be blindly followed when circumstances change and the base assumptions are flawed, then the results can be disastrous. 'The Charge of the Light Brigade' in 1854 in the Crimean War illustrates what can happen when people obey orders regardless of an obvious error and despite the obvious consequences, as the English poet Alfred Lord Tennyson described so eloquently in his poem of that title.

Complicated systems are characterised by a little more uncertainty. Here, cause and effect are still related, but it is not obvious exactly how. In these systems, there may be more than one answer and there is generally a need for expert judgement.

Modern medicine falls into this category. If we have repeated severe headaches, there are a number of possible causes. Relying on self-diagnosis from the internet (a 'simple' approach) would be unwise. We need to visit a doctor and have diagnostic tests in order to pinpoint the problem and come up with the best treatment.

Complicated systems lend themselves to in-depth review and analysis. Subject matter expertise and expert knowledge are critical. It helps to look outwards at what others with similar experience are doing, in order to develop ideas on what constitutes best practice.

People have come to expect that the vast majority of situations are addressable as though part of a complicated system. From this perspective, all problems, from world poverty to global warming, could be solved if we could only bring the right expertise to bear. But experts have limitations. They cannot foretell the future and are focused on their own area of speciality. In the real world most issues are not so closely defined.

Complex systems are typical of what we increasingly experience in everyday life. These are systems with a host of interacting variables, where boundary conditions are constantly changing, and where there is rarely complete agreement on what the situation is or even what constitutes success or failure. They are inherently ambiguous and open to different interpretations from different perspectives.

In such systems, it is very difficult to find straightforward linkages between cause and effect. While there is always a relationship, it is rarely obvious at the outset. Think about how cities grow, how the natural world evolves: typically, patterns emerge only in retrospect, emerging 'from the mist' as circumstances develop. This is an experience that most of us are familiar with: for example, the pattern and meaning of our own lives, our families, our communities and our societies generally only becomes clear with the passage of time, when we are able to put things into perspective and look back.

With complex systems, there is no one recipe for success. We have to try things out to learn what works. We need to stand back and see how things develop rather than force the pace. In this kind of system it helps to interact and discuss the situation with a wide variety of people rather than try and solve problems in isolation. Diverse perspectives provide the opportunity for creativity, new ideas and developing a fuller understanding of the bigger picture.

Complex systems are not easy to deal with. They take time to address, and successful resolution requires a degree of patience and perseverance which many do not possess. Many people prefer the apparent certainty of a quick answer, even when it may be wrong.

Chaotic systems are at the most uncertain end of the spectrum. Here, there is no evident relationship between cause and effect but rather an apparent randomness. What happens is due to chance. The behaviour of a chaotic system is impossible to predict, since even tiny changes in start conditions can result in different outcomes.

Our tendency to look for meaning in everything means we may underestimate the role of chance, looking for explanations that don't exist. In *Thinking Fast and Slow*, Daniel Kahneman describes how salesmen who had been rewarded as consistently good performers for exceeding their targets three years in a row may have just been lucky. According to physicist Stephen Hawking, even Einstein was mistaken in believing that chance had no part in explanations of the universe. Consideration of black holes suggests that, on the contrary, the universe may be akin to a confusing game of dice in which sometimes the dice themselves vanish and disappear from view.

What is the best way then to deal with chaotic systems? Conventional wisdom is that autocratic, directive leadership is needed to bring order out of chaos: act first, prioritise obedience, ask questions later. An example sometimes quoted is that of New York Mayor Giuliani, who took charge in the chaos that followed the 9/11 attack.

The risk, however, is that this command and control style can become the norm. What is effective in an emergency situation is likely to be conterproductive later when the challenge is to sort out complex issues requiring dialogue and debate. There is a history of 'strong' leaders who claim to have 'the answer' achieving power in this command and control way. Once people have a taste for power and being in charge, it can be difficult to persuade them to loosen it.

The most logical response to genuine randomness would be to accept fate and do our best to prepare ourselves for all eventualities. Many religions have this perspective, and Buddhism has a particularly impressive track record in this respect. Who could ever forget the calm demeanour of the thirteen Thai boys and their coach from the Wild Boars soccer team who had become trapped deep in a cave in June 2018, had no idea whether they would be rescued, and could only wait, hope and pray?

'Hard to classify' systems In practice, real-life situations rarely fall neatly into any of the four categories of the systems model. Different system types can be 'live' at the same time, making it hard to know which is the principal driver.

It can be difficult to know how to categorise a situation. A 'ready to cook' microwave meal illustrates well the direct 'cause and effect' characteristics of a simple system, but what about following a recipe from a cookbook? Is this a simple or complicated system – or does it lie somewhere in between? It is hard to say. It depends on a host of factors: the quality of the cook, availability of ingredients, standard of kitchen equipment, nature of the recipe, time available, and the expected quality of the outcome.

This can limit the usefulness of the systems framework as an everyday guide for how to behave, as to do this properly we would need to be able to categorise precisely each situation we encounter, and that's not as easy as it might first appear.

To further muddy the waters, if we were to apply a systems model literally to each situation we come across, we would have to continually adjust our approach: obedient one minute, challenging the next; autocratic on one occasion, involving the next; encouraging dialogue at one time, punishing those who speak out the next. Chopping and changing our style in this way risks adding to uncertainty.

Psychological approaches

So while logic is helpful, it's not the whole story. In many situations, our approach to uncertainty is shaped primarily by psychological considerations, in particular our desire to feel that we remain in control. There are a number of psychological strategies which people follow in order to do this, and these are summarised in the schematic diagram below.

We call these 'Richmor Strategies'. They are a key component of an overall framework for dealing with uncertainty that we have termed the 'Richmor Framework', which we develop further in the chapters that follow.

Defensive: A defensive strategy is the default approach that, in our experience, people use the most often.

In this strategy, our priority is to protect ourselves psychologically. This allows us to maintain our composure and not be overcome by anxiety or overwhelmed with data. We do this in a number of ways, the most important of which is to minimise the amount of new information we process, blocking out what we cannot cope with or do not want to hear. Taken to extremes, it can be a strategy of denial. But on an everyday level, it may just mean listening less often to the news or engaging less with the many platforms that bring breaking news information to us.

In our dealings with others, a defensive strategy means that, in general, we continue to act in ways that are already familiar, focusing on tried and tested behaviours that we understand and that we believe are likely to be effective.

• The great advantage of this strategy is that it keeps effort to a minimum by reducing information processing and the need to think too deeply for ourselves.

• It saves time and reduces uncertainty by providing immediate answers and ready-made solutions, helping us feel safe and secure.

• It also encourages us to be realistic and to accept that there are many things likely to be outside our control.

This strategy works well in situations where the problems and challenges turn out to be similar to those we have encountered in the past or where we have little power to change or influence things. Our societies, organisations and institutions generally reinforce the status quo and encourage us as individuals to adopt this way of looking at the world. Obviously this strategy is much less effective in circumstances which are different from the past, where our own response can make a difference, or where fine judgements and decisions are necessary.

Not surprisingly, there are risks in a VUCA world in adopting this strategy. Our actions and behaviours may turn out to be suboptimal for the evolving situation, not fitting new evidence and facts as they become available. Opportunities can be missed. We may eventually find ourselves at the mercy of changed circumstances as a consequence of having given up our freedom to learn and our possibilities for shaping the future.

We may have taken control of ourselves in the short term, but at the price of losing control over the longer period.

Disrupting: When we adopt a 'disrupting' strategy, our aim is to gain control by attempting to 'shift the goalposts' and rewrite the rules. We do this by challenging the current status quo and assumptions – and by refusing to accept the situation as presented. There may be a raft of reasons why we choose to adopt a disruptive stance: intellectual, political, ethical or even personal. More often than not, though, disruption is fuelled by emotion, generally anger that things are not as they should be. People may feel that they have little choice but to disrupt the status quo – or some of those who are disaffected may be driven by a desire to gain power.

Disruption is generally resisted by organisations and institutions who are the custodians of current systems and processes and who believe they would lose out under a new order. Consequently, disrupting strategies nearly always require the intelligent use of power and influence to shift the perceptions of others.

• Difficult conversations and negotiations may be required, alliances formed, bargains struck, deals done, communications reframed, history rewritten.

• Disrupting strategies are not for the faint-hearted. Courage, confidence and resilience are required.

• They usually require a lot of effort because it takes time and energy to get involved in this way and it is not possible to stand on the sidelines. It may mean taking an unpopular stand on the basis of incomplete information.

Disruption can be damaging without an understanding of the bigger picture, without heed for the consequences, or solely to further personal ambitions. Demeaning others, or distorting or misrepresenting facts, are not helpful in the long run.

On the other hand, responsible disruption, where the principal motive is to catalyse change which is in line with a broader vision and the good of the whole, can be a potent force for change. Responsible disruption involves taking calculated risks where the consequences of differing courses of action are thought through in advance in order to minimise unnecessary damage.

Disrupting approaches are important in a VUCA world when we need to find ways of breaking from habits and routines designed for different circumstances and another world order. They work less well when the cost of change and the disruption that it inevitably causes are greater than the benefits that are likely to be felt.

Accepting: With an accepting strategy, we accept that in an uncertain world much of what happens will lie outside our control. Rather than wasting our efforts on things we can do nothing about, we focus our attention instead on what we can control, in particular our own reactions and responses.

• We choose to let go of matters which may have preoccupied us in the past.

• We focus on our inner being and how we manage ourselves in response to the immediate situation.

This is essentially a spiritual approach. The accepting strategy is most appropriate in environments, where much of what happens is random and essentially unpredictable. Many of the world's religions operate partially in this domain.

The strategy operates with an orientation on the 'present'. Mindfulness, which encourages us to become deeply aware of our own thoughts and feelings and to observe them non-judgementally, is a key element, helping us to develop self-control and reduce our level of stress. Once we have a clear understanding of our inner selves, it is easier to make conscious choices about how to respond to situations rather than reacting impulsively.

There is evidence to suggest that those who are able to keep their self-composure in uncertain situations are likely to be more effective at leading others through complex change, and they are less likely to be personally affected by stress. They also seem to be well suited to coping with extreme situations involving personal danger and risk.

Exploring: The focus in this strategy is on trying to discover 'the truth', on the premise that once we develop a clearer understanding of a situation, we are in a better position both to control it and take advantage of opportunities.

This is a scientific, experimental and evidence-based approach. Curiosity lies at the heart of this paradigm. Those who are particularly attracted to it share a desire to try to understand, as far as possible, what is going on and how things could be influenced and improved. There is an unwillingness to accept that what happens depends solely on fate and factors outside one's control.

This approach makes strong demands on people. We need the confidence to think for ourselves and the courage to try new things. We must be open-minded, curious, prepared to keep our options open and not to jump to premature conclusions. It requires us to manage anxiety and be willing to change our minds. Sometimes it means we have to face up to unpleasant realities. Usually it means we have to be ready to take personal ownership and responsibility for action.

• An 'exploring' approach works best where there is the time available to do it properly and a degree of psychological maturity.

• People must be prepared to tolerate periods of uncertainty and ambiguity in exchange for the possibility of finding sustainable, longer-term solutions.

• It requires intelligence, education, and a social environment which tolerates differences. It also demands patience.

Over the long haul, exploratory strategies have proved to be very effective in reducing uncertainty by improving our levels of understanding. Once we understand, things seem simpler. Evidence-based approaches have been adopted by leading scientists, engineers and innovators over the years and have transformed the world.

Imposing: If we choose an 'imposing' strategy, our approach is to take control of the situation by putting into place our own view of what the future should be.

We do this through the use of power and influence, taking charge of 'shaping the future' in line with how we think it should be. We believe that we have a responsibility to make things happen, and are accountable for the results.

On a personal basis, we adopt an 'imposing' strategy when we rely on self-discipline; for example, if we decide to lose weight by going on an exercise regime and watching our diet.

When dealing with others, 'imposing' is the default strategy for many people who are in positions of power and authority, particularly those who are responsible for turning a drifting situation around; for example, a new CEO brought in to revitalise an organisation. Typically vision, mission and values are renewed, strategies developed, targets set, and detailed plans actioned. A less benign example would be an autocratic politician determined to implement his or her own view of an ideal world.

In an environment of uncertainty, there are always practical challenges associated with an 'imposing' strategy:

• Firstly, what happens if the vision turns out to be wrong or impractical? The vision may have been set without sufficient analysis, circumstances might change, or other possibilities may emerge. In these situations it could prove difficult to change course.

• Secondly, have the resources needed to impose the change been assessed realistically? Even losing weight, for example, is not easy – it takes imagination, willpower, self-belief, technical knowledge and self-discipline. Very often, things turn out to be more difficult than anticipated and the resources and capabilities required end up being greater than expected.

• Thirdly, will people do as they are told and go along with it?

Despite these issues and challenges, the judicious use of 'imposing' strategies is important in times of uncertainty. Things get done. The biggest risk is that there can be a tendency to 'double down' when faced with changing circumstances – and to use power to get our way quickly rather than rethink or adjust our tactics. We get so focused on driving home 'solutions', there is rarely enough time to listen to – and learn from – feedback.

In summary, in the face of uncertainty we adopt a number of psychological strategies to help us retain a sense of control. Which strategy is the most appropriate and effective in practice depends on both our own personality and the exact circumstances, but our assertion would be that the optimal strategy depends primarily on the level of uncertainty, as we discuss in the next chapter.

CHAPTER 4

The Richmor Model

'It may be impossible to be in control of events and circumstances, but it is possible to learn how to feel we are in control of ourselves and moving in a direction we want,' said Terri.
'But is that the right direction?' asked Richard.

A journey to uncertainty …

Driving through the prairies on the Trans-Canada Highway is the experience of a lifetime. Going from east to west, you travel for hours through Manitoba and Saskatchewan. Flat, rural, but beautiful. Brilliant yellow canola flowers, blue skies, fluffy white clouds and endless horizons. Mile after mile of wheatfields. Very few towns, widely separated. Long, straight roads as far as the eye can see. There is variation, but by and large the sense you have is of an environment that seems to go on for ever.

As you progress through Alberta, the environment begins to change. Suddenly, up ahead, the outline of the Rockies looms into view. A vertical wall of rock emerging from the plains. A series of increasingly high peaks extending into the distance, gradually disappearing into the clouds and mist. Snowcapped mountains at the highest levels. As you drive further towards them, the temperature starts to change and the light takes on a different quality. There are more clouds, more shadows.

As you progress deeper into the mountains, the landscape becomes ever more varied. Rivers, streams, lakes and wooded areas are evident, as well as the steep terrain. While the scenery is more exciting, the journey is more risky. The weather is variable and unpredictable. The roads are narrow and, at the highest levels, where there is ice and snow, there is the possibility of sliding or skidding. It's harder to know where you are headed as the sun is not always visible and the roads are winding.

This scenery also goes on for a long time; much more varied and dramatic than the prairies, and more dangerous. After navigating through one set of peaks, you come across another even more daunting range. This goes on for hundreds of miles with no end in sight until – suddenly – you emerge to see the magnificent blue Pacific Ocean coastline of British Columbia.

What a metaphor this journey is for the VUCA environment and the way our world has changed over the last few years – the predictable prairies, where we can anticipate easily what comes next, suddenly giving way to the more challenging and unpredictable mountains, swathed in cloud and mist, a seemingly endless set of unknown challenges. The same mountain looks different from every angle and perspective, and in the hills, weather conditions are volatile and can change rapidly. Navigating the same mountain is a different proposition in different weather conditions.

The Richmor Model

We have used this metaphor to develop our own mental model for conceptualising uncertainty, which we have called the Richmor Model.

In this world, we journey from the Richmor Plains, where life is comparatively straightforward, to the Richmor Range, where life is more complex and we face a number of different uncertainty challenges. Whereas in the plains we are able to spend our time in cruise control, navigating our way through these mountains of uncertainty requires more attention.

This way of thinking takes a broad view of uncertainty. We have entered a period of far-reaching and fundamental technogical, geopolitical and social change, facing situations unlike any we have encountered before. There is also turbulence and polarisation in the political environment, which further increases uncertainty.

Our model conceptualises uncertainty as a continuum rather than the series of discrete steps and categories we saw in the systems model. We have used quite general markers. At the 'certain' end of the scale, situations are straightforward, predictable and stable; at the other extreme, we find random systems, driven by chance, where we can expect the unexpected. The middle of the uncertainty scale is characterised by complex systems, ambiguity and volatility.

How does this model incorporate the five psychological strategies for dealing with uncertainty – defensive, disrupting, accepting, exploring and imposing – that we described earlier?

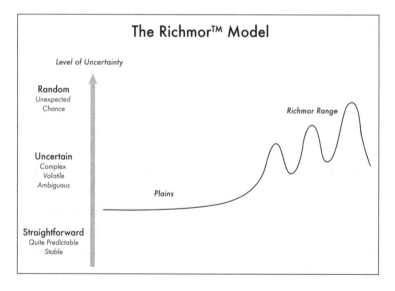

When we are travelling through relatively stable situations, the Richmor Plains, a 'defensive strategy' can save a lot of effort and keep anxiety to a minimum. This is because we stick with tried and trusted ways of behaving and spend a limited amount of energy and effort in scanning the environment for signs of change. Once we reach the Richmor Range, though, this strategy may no longer be the most sensible.

We can best illustrate this and how all the various strategies fit by looking at one of the mountains in the Richmor Range – let's call it the Richmor Ridge – and mapping the different psychological strategies from the Richmor Framework we discussed in the last chapter onto it, as shown in the schematic below.

Adopting our default **defensive** psychological strategy would imply that we refuse to accept that much has changed, and instead we operate as if the situation continues as it was.

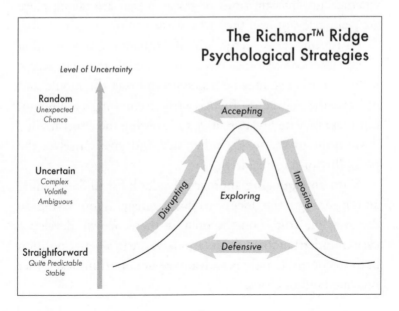

63

We stay at the same level on the ridge. Why make changes when there is no need to?

This is like trying to reach the other side of a mountain by simply walking around the outside at the same level rather than having to climb to the top and descend. It may work on some occasions, but sometimes there is little alternative to climbing.

When we choose to adopt a **disrupting** strategy, we are taking a very different approach. We challenge the status quo and any underlying assumptions. In doing so we effectively move up the Richmor Ridge. We make things less certain than they were.

In order to create the space for a new order, we start by calling the existing order into question. We ask if the rules, principles and procedures that are characteristic of the existing situation are still appropriate and fit for purpose; we challenge the views of experts with whom we disagree; we challenge whether any investigations or research that are taking place are really relevant or if they are a waste of time.

Disrupting takes energy. Still, if a situation is deteriorating – and either complacency has set in or people refuse to accept reality – challenge may be necessary to break the mould and unfreeze the status quo. There is a risk in climbing a mountain, but there may be no alternative to investing the effort needed if we want to get to the other side and give ourselves the possibility of starting afresh.

With an **exploring** approach, we look for understanding and meaning. The focus in this strategy is on trying to discover 'the truth', on the premise that once we develop a clearer understanding of a situation, we are in a better position both to control it and take advantage of opportunities. Order is created out of chaos.

Unfortunately, an exploring strategy increases uncertainty before order is established. The process of discovery is rarely smooth, and at times there may be more questions than answers. It can move us both up and down the Richmor Ridge. The time spent in reconnaissance and planning – attempting to find the best way down – requires patience. It can also provoke anxiety.

With an **accepting** strategy, we are generally operating at the height of uncertainty, the top of the Richmor Ridge, where we accept that there is much we cannot influence.

Our focus, instead, must be on safety and emotional control. We keep to the same level on the ridge and ensure we remain alert and stay protected, all the time monitoring the situation and being prepared to take action when the weather improves.

When we adopt an **imposing** strategy, we use power and influence to create order from chaos. Generally we have a clear idea of the solution, and we organise to achieve that. This moves us down the Richmor Ridge.

Indeed, imposing strategies allow for speedy implementation without the need for much debate or discussion. However, if the wrong slope of the mountain has been chosen, it makes it harder to get to the right place. And there is always the possibility of crashing.

The Richmor Steps

The next stage is to combine these psychological strategies with the logical systems thinking we described earlier so that the model not only helps us to feel in control but also shows us the best actions to take to be effective.

We have developed a simple, four-stage approach, which we call the Richmor Steps, that can be followed through major periods of uncertainty, and which we believe should work in the majority of such situations. The stages are general rather than specific.

Our lives have a substantive element of habit and routine. For this reason, we don't see the Richmor Steps as dictating how people should live their entire lives but do believe there is merit in this approach becoming a habit during uncertain times. They are intended more as a set of 'loosely held principles' than a code of rigid rules. This is partly because the Richmor Steps reflect an overall mindset and philosophy. Personal leadership is at its heart: taking personal responsibility and ownership for dealing with uncertainty, accepting that while we may be unable to control what is happening around us, we do have control over how we choose to respond to it.

We recognise that people need the 'soft' skills to back this up, including ways of thinking, dealing with others, and managing themselves, and we describe these later in the book. We also recognise that it is important that society and organisations are supportive and encouraging of those who act in this way and that they are not set up in ways that make it impossible. We cover that in the final chapter.

We make a number of assumptions:

• In practice most of the uncertain situations we are likely to come across will be complex, and need rethinking and reframing.

• Solutions are rarely obvious, so thinking time should be factored in.

• Putting our chosen solution into practice is usually difficult and needs attention.

We have also taken the view that a straightforward, consistent approach is desirable because constantly chopping and changing our strategies, tactics and behaviours to fit the exact circumstances in which we find ourselves is not only difficult for us and disturbing to others, but risks adding to the confusion and making matters worse.

Although the overall approach is flexible, sometimes there is not the time to follow all the stages proposed in detail. In an emergency, it is impossible to conduct a thorough strategic review or to research all the options and possibilities in depth. For example, the decision to land a crippled American airliner on the Hudson when a bird strike disabled its engines had to be made in a few seconds. Prior experience and professional judgement were critical.

How best to describe the model? Well, let us imagine a situation where we feel 'stuck', doing things in the same way that we always have and realising that we are not as effective as we used to be. Circumstances are changing, and the future is far from clear. Unexpected events continually catch us off-balance and frustrate our plans. What is the best way to change this situation?

Research by clinical psychologist Dr James Prochaska, and his colleagues, shows how the process of fundamental behaviour change typically evolves. It can take years. We can go through long periods of thinking – what they term 'pre-contemplation' and 'contemplation' – before we get round to action. The pattern usually involves learning intellectually about the problem – a process which in itself may involve repeated exposure to relevant information before being accepted – followed by an emotional dawning that we can not carry on in the same way because it is having an impact on ourselves and others. If we feel confident enough to try something out, we make a small change and if this works we will try to make it a habit.

In thinking through the Richmor Steps, we have taken this research into account but have tried to design an approach that will speed up the process. During periods of uncertainty we don't always have the luxury of time. Our perspective is that when we are 'stuck', we are generally operating at a lower level on the Richmor Ridge, 'going through the motions' and following practices that are no longer effective. In order to free ourselves, we need to follow a process that will effectively move us up and over the hill.

Critically, we have to start thinking more strategically, to make sense of the situation in terms of what we really want to achieve, before testing out some options and putting them into practice. The four stages of the approach are shown in the diagram below.

Step 1. *Making Time to Think.* The first stage is to carve out some time to think and reflect. Initially many people will say this is impossible. Their volume of day-to-day operational activities, responsibilities and duties, leaves them no capacity for anything else. Whilst this may be the situation for some, after years of working in this field with many extremely busy individuals we have yet to come across a case where, with some imagination and sacrifice, this cannot be achieved. If we cannot take charge of our time, we cannot take charge of our lives.

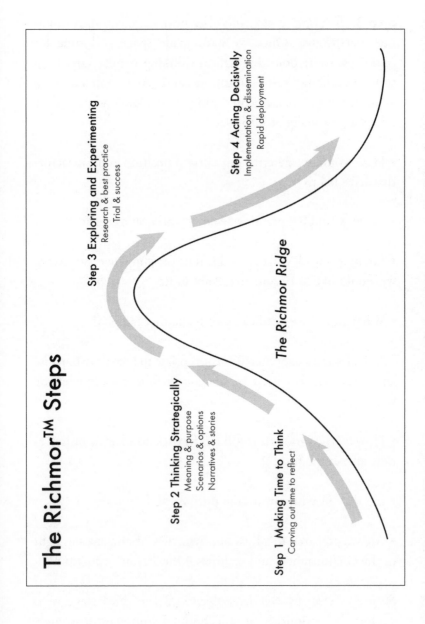

The Richmor™ Steps

Step 3 Exploring and Experimenting
Research & best practice
Trial & success

Step 4 Acting Decisively
Implementation & dissemination
Rapid deployment

Step 2 Thinking Strategically
Meaning & purpose
Scenarios & options
Narratives & stories

Step 1 Making Time to Think
Carving out time to reflect

The Richmor Ridge

Step 2. *Thinking Strategically.* The next stage is to put things into perspective. Once we have made space and time for ourselves, some objective critical thinking is necessary. It's a time to challenge, test assumptions, and take a cool, hard look at our situation, focusing on the big picture and understanding how we personally fit into that.

• How would we describe our current position and the factors that have led to it?

• What would happen if we were to carry on as we are?

• Looking ahead, what is our ideal future and what is the story we would like to be able to tell about it?

• What would we need to do to make that happen?

This is also the stage when it is appropriate to take time to pause and assess whether what we are considering is really what we want.

• How do the various possibilities fit with how we see ourselves now and in the future?

• Do they fit with our overall purpose and values?

• Are we prepared to adjust our own view of ourselves in light of the circumstances and realities of the various scenarios?

Step 3. *Exploring and Experimenting.* The third stage is to explore the options. In an uncertain environment, it is rarely possible to find ready-made, 'off the shelf' solutions; rather we have to develop unique alternatives that fit our specific circumstances and move us in the right direction.

This approach is most effective when we do not work in isolation but in conjunction with others, in an environment of collaboration, communication and creativity. Dialogue, discussion and interactivity – and a bit of competitive spirit – are also helpful; looking at what others are doing and current best practice saves time. Generally it is best to develop a number of options and to try them out so that we do not have all our eggs in one basket. Conducting such small-scale trials that can afford to fail without serious consequences gives us the chance to see what options work best in practice.

A precise project plan with everything spelt out in detail rarely works as we cannot be certain how the environment might change in the course of the plan's execution. The principles of emergent change – the kind which happens naturally if the circumstances are favourable – apply as we work to create the conditions where creativity and innovation can flourish. It is an approach described as 'trial and success' because we focus on finding and backing winning approaches rather than investing our resources and efforts in trying to change, block or stop less successful initiatives.

Step 4. *Acting Decisively.* Having found something that we think should work, the final step is to implement this decisively and rapidly. It is at this stage that we need to develop a clear implementation plan, breaking things down into manageable chunks with clear objectives, targets, activities and responsibilities.

A SIMPLE ILLUSTRATION OF THE RICHMOR STEPS

Imagine you have been working in a well-paid job for many years but are beginning to feel stuck. While the job is okay, you wonder whether it is the best option. You are uncertain what to do next. What might you consider using the Richmor Steps?

Step 1. You would carve time out of your busy life to take stock. Often when we are hard at work the last thing we want to do is take a step back, but until we do so, nothing will change.

Step 2. You would consider the big picture. Is the job still what I want? How is it changing? What am I really looking for? What are my strengths and weaknesses? Is it really worth moving? Do I want to leave or not?

Step 3. You would take the time to explore alternatives, researching online, talking to others, taking advice and checking out potential employers. You might experiment.

Step 4. You would act decisively once you were clear on what you wanted and what was possible, targeting applications to specific roles in a planned campaign.

CHAPTER 5

Time to Think

'There's no such thing as work–life balance. Work is part of life, not something you can or should look at separately,' said Terri. 'When am I going to get time to play my saxophone again then?' asked Richard.

The time for 'time out'

It is nearly always challenging to find ways to carve time out of our busy lives in order to reflect and strategise. What situations, then, merit us taking a step back? In what circumstances is it really necessary?

Let us start with the most obvious. When we are faced with a sudden change, a crisis or discontinuity in our lives – for example moving to a new house, a new job, the loss of a close relative – taking time out to reassess where we are and what we should be doing is a natural reaction. Since we do not have the option of continuing in the same way as in the past, it makes sense to take the time to work out what we should do next.

Many would agree that taking time out is extremely worthwhile when we are faced with periods of high uncertainty, turbulence or challenge. When things are changing at a rapid pace we need to take stock and re-evaluate on a fairly frequent basis, to make sure we keep on top of what is happening. Regular review is advisable.

What, though, if things seem relatively stable? Is it really necessary to take time out then? For large periods of our lives, we are likely to feel that things are relatively unchanging. We get into daily routines and habits, become used to particular ways of behaving, and comfortable with what we are doing.

It is analogous to driving across the plains. The road is straight and flat. We are making progress. There is no need to check the map. During these stable times it can be difficult to persuade people to 'take stock' when things seem to be going well. What is the need? Why waste time?

Unfortunately, our perceptions of stability can be illusory. The biggest risk is complacency, not realising that the world is changing and that this may have a major impact on us in the future unless we are prepared to modify our current behaviours. We can get stuck in a situation where our options are more limited than they need be, because we did not register what was actually happening and take action early enough. Climate change is an interesting example of this at the global level.

We believe that finding a way to take 'time out' is always a good idea, even in apparently stable circumstances, particularly when it comes to our most important undertakings. At a minimum, it is essential to ask the question, 'What is likely to happen if we continue as we are?' It is important to get into the habit of taking a step back and looking at the bigger picture, even if things appear to be going well. The risks of being unaware and caught out in a volatile, uncertain world are too high.

There is always time for a drink with your friends …

What is the best way to do this? And how can we find the time in our busy lives to put this into practice?

Experience has taught us to be more sanguine about 'busyness' than we used to be. It is surprising how it is possible to make space when we really have to – and if we really want to.

Some of the most interesting sessions we run on our leadership development programmes are about how people prioritise their time. Being busy seems to have become a 'badge of honour' for many people. The starting point is generally a conversation about how busy everyone is, how information technology and the 'always on' culture are making things worse, and how there is never enough time in the day to do all the things we need to do. Even discussing the topic makes some people anxious. Occasionally, they will comment that they do not really have time for a session like this, as they could be getting on with their proper job.

The fundamental challenge around time management is how we manage ourselves within a fixed resource – twenty-four hours a day. Although time is inelastic, fixed, we are not. To illustrate the point we use a well-known exercise, which we have been informed is similar to an experiment originally described by the anthropologist and cybernetician Gregory Bateson. The exercise was later popularised by the American educator Stephen R. Covey and is now widely used.

We stand in front of the group with a large transparent jar, which we then fill with coloured soft juggling balls. We ask them to tell us when it is full and they duly oblige. At this point we reach under the table and pull out a number of marbles which we pour into the jar in the spaces that are left. We ask the class if the jar is now full. They generally laugh, and say yes.

Once again, we reach under the table. This time we pull out a bag of flour. By now there is usually a knowing laugh in the group. 'Is it full?' we ask. 'No!' they reply this time, and we confirm their insight by emptying the bag of flour into the jar on top of the juggling balls and marbles.

In our debrief we ask participants to imagine that the transparent jar represents the fixed amount of time there is in the day. The large balls represent their major life objectives, the marbles their day-to-day duties and responsibilities, and the flour all the trivial everyday things they have to manage. The exercise shows that provided we know what our major responsibilities are and focus on these first, then it's generally possible to carry out our duties and still have the space to deal with everyday matters.

But what happens if we do not have this focus? Our tendency is to do all the immediate things first – in other words, to fill up the jar with the flour. Self-evidently, if we do that, there will not be space for anything else. We have clogged up the jar before we have even started.

The most entertaining part of this insightful exercise is yet to come. Having been through the debrief, we ask again if the jar is full. This time the group is a little unsure. We reach beneath the table and pull out a bottle of wine. Removing the top, we pour the wine into an increasingly messy-looking jar, but it all goes in. 'Which only goes to show,' we say, 'there's always time for a drink with your friends!'

The most fun we had with this activity was with the senior management of a well-known whiskey company in Ireland. We managed to obtain an empty bottle of their most expensive whiskey, retailing at many hundreds of euros, and filled it with a cheap substitute. When we pulled out the bottle for the final part of the exercise, opened it and poured it into the jar there was an audible intake of breath from the assembled group as they noticed the expensive label.

They never forgot the message!

The need for focus

While time may be inelastic, how we choose to fill it is not. What can we learn from research on time management? Most of this research is carried out on people working in organisations. This provides a fairly straightforward way of identifying which approaches tend to be the most successful, as the strategies used by top and average performers can be directly compared. Much of the research emphasises the importance of being focused, with two main lessons emerging:

Focus on strategic priorities. Most people tend to get distracted by whatever seems important at the time, or get bogged down in what they believe to be unyielding duties and responsibilities. Those who are more successful are much more purposeful in their approach and find ways of managing their lives so they don't feel that everything they do is dictated by day-to-day operational activities and tasks.

The best way to go about this is to make sure we are clear about our strategic objectives and priorities and are genuinely personally committed to them. One of the priorities should be making sure we have some regular space in the diary for reflection. We need to be mindful of how we spend our time, ensuring that what we do fits with our overall objectives, and that we learn how to pursue our goals systematically and methodically.

LEARNING TO PLAY THE SAXOPHONE
Story (Richard)

When I was ten years old, I put up my hand in a music class when the teacher asked if anyone wanted to learn to play the recorder. I was doing my best to cultivate a tough image at the time, and only put my hand up as a joke. Playing the recorder was not seen as cool. However, the teacher took me seriously and enrolled me. Completely unexpectedly, I turned out to be quite good at it and a year later ended up playing a solo in front of hundreds of people. Unfortunately, my career ended abruptly thereafter when I changed school.

Fast forward half a century. For years I had harboured a secret desire to play jazz saxophone. That was cool. If I could play the recorder, perhaps I could learn to play alto or tenor sax? Unfortunately, I never believed I had the time to do it. To learn how to play a musical instrument takes a lot of practice. My life was just too busy. I had too many commitments.

The arrival of my 'Senior Bus Pass' through the post gave me a wake-up call. If I didn't start now, I never would. I went out the same day and bought a saxophone. I was committed. After a month of frustration (I was trying to teach myself with the mouthpiece upside down and couldn't get a note out of it), I found a great teacher (thanks, Ben!) and, to my surprise, discovered that it was relatively easy to carve out the time to practise. I just watched less TV. And one of the proudest moments of my life was passing my Grade 8 exam six years later.

Do not take on too much. Heike Bruch, Professor of Leadership at the University of St Gallen in Switzerland, and Sumantra Ghoshal, former Professor of Strategic and International Management at London Business School, studied the behaviour of 'busy managers' over many years. They noted that many were always rushing from meeting to meeting, checking their email constantly, and 'fighting fires'. However, while they may have thought they were attending to important matters, in reality they were just spinning their wheels, with fully 90 per cent squandering their time on all sorts of ineffective activities. The 10 per cent who were effective managed their time carefully and spent it on purposeful, committed activities.

Recent research has confirmed these findings. People who spread themselves too thinly don't achieve the same level of performance as those who focus on doing a few things well. Management theorist Morten Hansen reports that top performers in organisations work fewer hours than average performers but are obsessive about achieving a really high standard in what they do. They are passionate about their work and purposeful about how they go about it.

The psychiatrist Edward Hallowell has argued that the problem of trying to do too much is currently so pervasive that a dysfunctional pattern of behaviour has emerged, which he calls ADT (Attention Deficit Trait). This arises when people become so overwhelmed with information and data that they are unable to focus properly on anything, rarely completing a task and generally appearing stressed and ineffective. Yet the evidence is clear that the most productive time managers focus on one activity at a time, do it well, and then move on – rather than doing a lot of things badly.

The fallacy of work–life balance

We have serious reservations about the concept of 'work–life balance'. This idea is based on the premise that 'work' and 'life' are different entities and are set up in opposition to each other. Yet work is integral to our sense of well-being and purpose in our lives, not something separate. We are more likely to feel fulfilled if we think of work as a meaningful part of our lives rather than something to be endured.

What is more, the definition of 'work' is increasingly unclear. Does work only mean paid work as an employee? What about voluntary work? What about the social support and social care we provide for others?

The 'work–life balance' concept is also based on the premise that there is a strict boundary to what we call 'work'. However, the internet and technology are reshaping our ways of working, blurring those very boundaries. Too rigid a separation leads to inflexibility, by optimising only the work component of the system. For example, there is legislation in some European countries which prevents people from sending or answering emails outside office hours. By reducing flexibility and taking away individual choice, this risks making matters worse.

The idea that 'too much work' is what affects our ability to make space and time for ourselves is naïve. In most advanced economies, less than a third of our time is spent in paid employment and this proportion has been steadily reducing over the last century. The real issue is that the societal context has changed and we have much higher expectations of our lives, in particular how we spend our time when not at work. There are many more ways of spending our leisure time than in the past. For example, keeping up with social media – a phenomenon that did not exist twenty years ago – now takes up a lot of people's time.

At the same time, it is best to be realistic about the difficulties of maintaining a balanced life. There is no point in beating ourselves up about this. The belief that we will always be able to keep an ideal balance is illusory and impractical. There are times when workloads may peak, when emergencies occur at home, or when we are not in full health. To expect ourselves always to be in perfect balance is unrealistic. We are better off accepting that sometimes life can be very challenging – and the best we can do is to set aside some 'me time' every day.

There are also some life-cycle stages where, whatever the pressures of work, our personal and family commitments make it difficult to find adequate time for sleep, let alone time for ourselves.

The diagram on the facing page shows hypothetical examples of two life stages where there are often severe pressures on discretionary time: dual-career families with young children, and someone who is successful in mid-career undertaking multiple roles. Of course, the extent of any issue in practice depends on the exact circumstances, in particular how much support is available. The picture illustrates how different these circumstances can be from those typically encountered in early adulthood or later life.

The problem with busyness is not so much 'work–life balance' as feeling in control and taking responsibility for the whole of our lives. For this we need to have as much flexibility as possible to structure and order our time to fit our individual circumstances.

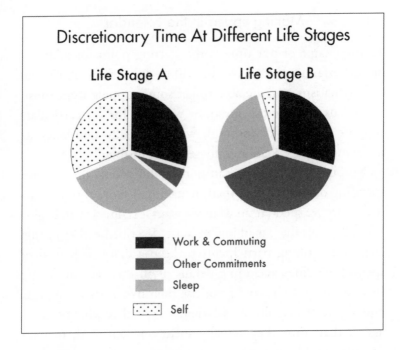

Life Stage A: time for self

Examples

- Early career as an independent adult

- Late career with few other commitments

Life Stage B: little time for self

Examples

- Dual-career family with young children

- Successful mid-career with multiple roles: parent, brother or sister, step-parent, respected professional, manager, do-it-yourself expert, community leader, part-time college learner, colleague, friend

Making space in the calendar

Taking charge of our time is the starting point for addressing uncertainty. If we have the will to do it, show a little bit of pragmatism, and are able to get some support from those around us and the organisations we work for (in particular, support for flexible working), we can usually find ways to make more space than initially seemed possible.

Keeping a diary so we can understand exactly how we are spending our time – and then managing it more ruthlessly to make sure we spend it on what we want – is one way to begin. We follow up the 'jar-filling' exercise described earlier in this chapter by asking participants to keep a diary of how they spend their time, including details of all their activities. We then ask them to list and prioritise their five or six main goals and objectives. Finally, we ask them to calculate what percentage of their time they actually spent on each of their main priorities and how much time was spent on other matters.

The results usually surprise our participants. Generally speaking, people spend much less time than they think on their priority objectives. Why might this be?

The primary reason is usually that participants had not really taken the time in the first place to clarify their strategic priorities, and if they did, they rarely considered these in the context of their lives as a whole. They hardly ever bothered to think deeply about how they were spending their time, often getting stuck into time-consuming activities (social media and TV being the worst culprits) or becoming easily distracted.

But there are other, deeper reasons too.

• Taking charge of our own time takes courage.

• Usually we have to drop something we were intending to do, reschedule it, or delegate it to someone else – in which case we have to learn to trust them.

• We have to be prepared to make sacrifices, changing our customs and habits.

• We have to accept that other people may criticise or evaluate us negatively for doing things differently – and we have to be tough enough to live with that.

• We may have to be prepared to say 'no' to other people's demands.

• We have to be prepared to be proactive, make our own decisions and trust our own judgement rather than going with the conventional wisdom.

• We have to be prepared, sometimes, to be 'less than perfect' or 'not liked'.

We also need to be more creative about how we value time and how we fill it.

• Are there activities we could cut, do differently or combine with others to make space for something else?

• Are there meetings that could be rescheduled, postponed, rearranged, cancelled or dropped altogether? Could some things be done virtually rather than requiring travel?

• Can we use technology to help us?

We have developed the habit of regularly reviewing our diaries to check whether what we planned is still relevant in our fast-changing environment, and to see if there is enough time and space left to give us flexibility. It is impossible to make the time to think strategically if every day is filled with meeting after meeting, preprogrammed totally in advance. It is important to schedule in 'reflective space' as well as 'activity'.

In our experience, the bigger risk is not the investment required to take time out and take stock, it is carrying on regardless in conditions that are volatile and changing. It is important to get into the habit of making space to reflect and think, even for a few minutes a day, and not get obsessed with completing detailed lists of activities and tasks.

So schedule some 'just doing nothing' time into the diary. It will not be time wasted.

CHAPTER 6
Thinking Strategically

'I can't see beyond my nose,' said Terri. 'That's because you're still wearing your reading glasses,' replied Richard.

The importance of seeing the big picture …

There's a scene in an episode of the TV comedy series *The Simpsons* where Homer is involved in a fierce argument with his wife and children. Becoming more and more frustrated and angry, he takes a piece of chalk and draws a white line on the floor directly in front of him. He then tells his wife Marge and their children that from now on they should stay on their side of the white line, and he will stay on his! At that point, the camera pans back rapidly and we (and Homer) realise that he has literally backed himself into a corner, where he has no space to manoeuvre. 'D'oh!' he says, slapping himself on the forehead as he realises the gravity of his error.

This vignette illustrates brilliantly what can happen in tricky situations if we simply react emotionally and don't think through the consequences of our actions. It is all too easy to behave in ways that close down our options and upset those around us. We are more likely to make sensible choices and speedy decisions 'in the moment' if we understand the bigger picture and how we fit into it. This also makes it less likely that we will overreact.

Indeed, in the instance described above, Homer Simpson might have benefited from some training in self-awareness and mindfulness, using the techniques of cognitive behavioural therapy (CBT). For example, the STOPP technique – sometimes called 'CBT in a nutshell' – can be used as an effective tool to help those who are feeling anxious or concerned to regain control of their emotions and put things into perspective. The steps are as follows:

Stop – pause for a moment;

Take a breath;

Observe how you are thinking and feeling;

Pull back and put things in perspective and, only after all this has been done,

Proceed. Think before you act.

As the writers of *The Simpsons* are only too aware, the positive side of reacting spontaneously is that it can be perceived as authentic, entertaining and (sometimes) endearing. It can be easier for us to relate to people who seem straightforward than to those who are more calculating. It is an example of what Israeli-American psychologist and economist Daniel Kahneman calls Type 1 thinking: fast, instinctive and emotional. But such thinking does not help us to be effective or make sound decisions in complex, uncertain situations. For those situations we need a slower, considered and thoughtful Type 2 approach.

Understanding the big picture is key to strategic thinking. It allows us to simplify things so we don't drown in the detail but instead see ourselves as part of a broader system. It is a widely valued quality. Shell, the international energy company, call this the helicopter quality – the ability to zoom in and out of a situation, seeing the big picture as well as simultaneously understanding all the relevant detail.

Taking stock

The starting point for strategic thinking is an objective assessment of our current circumstances. We take stock by pausing, stepping back, and looking at our current situation and environment as realistically and objectively as possible. Because by nature we are adaptable, we do not always notice significant changes that are happening around us. As the adage goes, 'the fish does not see the water it is swimming in'.

Our mental models are based on a whole series of assumptions, and sometimes these need to be checked. As time goes on, we become more confident about our underlying mental models, which can lead to either wisdom, or prejudice and bigotry, depending on the models' quality and whether or not they are challenged and reviewed. If we take steps to ensure that our models are continually updated and refreshed as new information and facts become available, we are less likely to build castles in the air when we try to think realistically and strategically.

Taking stock provides the opportunity to challenge and test assumptions and take a cool, hard look at our situation. This does not have to be a formal, lengthy process, and there are many ways that we can do this:

• Regularly finding the time to ask ourselves simple questions about what is going on, and how that makes us feel. What is really happening? How would we describe our current position and the factors that have led to it? What would someone else say about our situation? How important is it really in the grand scheme of things?

• Getting into the habit of spending a few minutes at the end of the day reviewing the main things that have happened to us. What do we think were the underlying circumstances? What did we do well? What could we have done differently, and what might all this mean?

• Sharing our experience in a structured way with our peers – for example through 'co-mentoring' with a colleague or facilitated sessions which encourage a climate of openness and psychological safety. Getting feedback from others.

If we need to take a more in-depth look at our own situation, a more structured process can be helpful. There are a number of routine, tried and trusted approaches that are used by organisations which we can borrow and adapt.

For example, if we want to understand more thoroughly what is happening in the outside world, we can take a look at how the context is changing from a **p**olitical, **e**conomic, **s**ocial, **t**echnological, **e**nvironmental and **l**egislative perspective. This is called a PESTEL analysis. We can ask:

• What trends can we see?

• What do we think is likely to happen in the future?

We might also want to look at our own situation in more depth using what organisations call a SWOT analysis (a re-view of **s**trengths, **w**eaknesses, **o**pportunities and **t**hreats). We could ask:

• What do we see as our current purpose and values?

- In that context, what do we see as our strengths and weaknesses?

- What are the opportunities and threats to achieving our objectives?

- What might happen if we were simply to continue as we are?

Imagining futures

Once we have taken stock, the really interesting part of the process can begin. Looking ahead, what do we see as our ideal future and what is the story we would really like to be able to tell about it? How do we see our part in this? What is our purpose?

Having a clear and meaningful sense of purpose makes a difference to our feelings of pride, happiness and well-being. It is a key part of our identity and enables us to focus on what is important by looking through a relevant lens. This helps us feel in control by reducing both information overload and anxiety in the context of the bigger picture.

We witnessed how powerful a sense of purpose can be when we were introducing a new performance management and development system to Irish Local Government. One young man looked a lot happier at the end of our workshop than he did at the beginning. We asked him why. 'I used to think my job was just cutting the grass,' he said. 'Now I understand that I am cutting the grass to keep things tidy and to make the Visitor Centre look more attractive to tourists. That encourages people to visit and spend their money here.

So what I am really doing is contributing to making Ireland a great place for tourists and boosting the economy.'

How we choose to define ourselves is very important. Evidence shows that we tend to act in ways that are consistent with our self-image. Christopher Bryan of Stanford University has run a number of experiments which confirm what successful sportspeople among others have known for years: how we think about ourselves makes a big difference to behaviours and outcomes. For example, citizens who think of themselves as 'voters' are more likely to vote than those who don't.

So we need to make sure that we keep our own sense of 'who we are' and our higher purpose up to date. We have to be prepared to adjust our own view of ourselves and who we are in light of changing circumstances and our own development. The psychologist Carl Jung pointed out that it was impossible to live the 'afternoon' of our lives according to the programme of the 'morning'. What matters to us when we are young may count for little as we get older, and what was true in our youth can become a lie in old age.

'Reframing' our identity and developing a new, meaningful sense of purpose is something that we are all capable of, though there is no single way of going about it. Even if we do not try to do it consciously, it is likely to happen anyway. Sometimes meaning, purpose and reframing of identity can be triggered by a shock or dramatic event; sometimes it emerges into our consciousness; sometimes we have no alternative; other times, like for our grass cutter, it may come out of the opportunity to think more deeply about things.

The more proactive we are about reframing, though, the better. It helps us get on with our lives. It makes more sense to be looking forward than looking back.

One way of doing this is to clarify our thinking about what an idealised future would look like. This is really a version of the 'what do I want to be when I grow up?' question. In attempting to look towards the future we find that an exercise called 'Newspaper Headlines' works particularly well. We ask people to imagine that it is a few years into the future and they see a news stand with the latest copy of a popular newspaper. On closer examination, they see that the entire paper is dedicated to a story about them. We then ask them to create the cover page of the newspaper, with the cover story headline, a list of feature articles, quotes from those who know them, a summary of the cover story with key milestones and events, and a picture to support the story.

People get enthused about this exercise. The real value, though, is not in the detail of the future vision, but in thinking through what this future vision implies for what they should do *right now*. The advantage of thinking strategically rather than making snap decisions is that once we have a good idea of what we want to achieve, we can then work out the implications of that for us *now*. Think forwards, reason backwards.

For example, if we realise that our true aspiration is to be an entrepreneur rather than being in employment, we might want to be much more proactive about exploring opportunities, making contacts, and thinking through how we could finance ourselves.

• We might recalibrate our attitudes towards risk.

• We might cultivate different friends.

• We might do some research.

• We might enrol on a course.

• We might change our image or dress style.

Imagining the future in this way also gives us an opportunity to reflect on our core values. This is about *how* we do things, rather than *what* we are trying to achieve. Arguably, this is even more important than our vision or purpose, since it is the main driver of our behaviours, including ethical behaviours, and generally remains quite constant over time. Even so, we may need to adapt, adjust and in particular re-prioritise our values to ensure they are consistent with our aspirations. As an illustration, in our entrepreneur example, we might decide that we need to pay more attention to 'being proactive' than we did when we were working in a different role that did not require proactivity.

In clarifying our values, we need to draw on all our experience, linking our principles, beliefs, preferences, capabilities and personality with the aspirations we have for the future. The aim is to end up with a few simple priorities which make sense in the context we are in – and which guide how we want to behave and work with others.

Developing stories

In uncertainty, we search for meaning. Once we have taken stock of the situation and considered our ideal future, we are in a great position to construct our own personal 'story' which we can use to explain things to ourselves and others.

A coherent, strategic narrative which links together past, present and future can be a wonderful guide for decision-making. It shows us how we fit into the bigger picture and gives us a template for understanding experiences, developing options, and evaluating alternative courses of action. It can be motivating and inspiring.

Once we have done the background thinking, it is time to develop a good story. Of course, we can develop this initially in private, but a story grows and evolves as we try it out. We can test our ideas with others we trust through conversation, email or even social media, adjusting and adapting as we get feedback until we eventually end up with a story that seems to work. This is done best in a climate in which we feel a sense of 'psychological safety' and where we are able to share our views openly.

DEVELOPING PERSONAL STORIES (Terri)

In 2013, I was asked to facilitate a 'story-telling' session for a major Irish company. They wanted to make sure that their values were well understood and brought to life through a process of personal story-telling. Their sales and marketing conference held in South Africa provided the ideal opportunity for putting this idea into practice.

Over 250 people attended the first stage of the workshop in a Cape Town hotel. Divided into groups of ten, each person was asked to tell a personal story about one of the values which demonstrated the value in action. There was a competitive, 'knock-out' process, first within the groups and then between them, which resulted in the three best stories being identified. Of course, as the story-tellers became more practised, their stories became better.

The entire group was then taken on a surprise tour of Robben Island, where they visited the prison where Nelson Mandela was held and the cell he lived in. It was an inspiring experience, reinforcing the importance of values and commitment.

Following the tour, the group repaired to the community hall on Robben Island, where the three winners gave their personal stories about the values. The atmosphere was electric and the impact powerful.

Stories and sense-making are powerful tools in helping us deal with uncertainty, but they are not without associated risks. Stories are most helpful when they are supported by evidence, tested and revised as new data emerges. It is important that we keep them under review, or else they can become little more than fabrication. If facts are suppressed so as not to spoil the story, such narratives can end up being used as propaganda. 'Fake news', based on emotional resonance or convenient fabrication rather than fact, is the outcome.

Testing thinking

In an uncertain world, events rarely unfold as we imagine. It does not help to continually bemoan the state of the world or the incompetence of others. While we can always work on shaping our own environment to a certain extent, we also need to keep our options open and flexible so we can adjust and adapt to the unexpected. We should also ensure that we have contingency plans in place in case things turn out completely differently than anticipated or planned.

How can we do this? Scenario planning is an established method for testing our ideas. It involves thinking objectively about different eventualities and working out the implications of each. By thinking things through in advance and preparing for a range of possibilities, it is easier to take decisive and rapid action when necessary.

In our deliberations, it's always useful to look at a 'worst case' scenario. This can be tricky. Professor Tali Sharot, an Israeli-British-American neuroscientist, describes research which shows that people have an inbuilt 'optimism bias', believing that the future will be much better than the past and present. They don't like to think of what might go wrong.

This positive tendency generally serves us well and keeps us healthy. Indeed, optimism may be crucial to our very existence: the evidence suggests that optimists live longer than pessimists. The American psychologist Martin Seligman argues that optimists are more resilient than pessimists. He notes that pessimists tend to believe that bad events will last a long time, will undermine everything they do, and are their own fault, whereas optimists tend to believe that defeat is just a temporary setback or challenge.

At the same time, Sharot points out that the optimism bias can be unhelpful when developing strategies to prepare us for all eventualities. There are occasions when our success depends on having a plan 'ready to roll' when faced with an emergency or crisis situation. 'Thinking the unthinkable' doesn't make it more likely to happen but it does help us to be prepared when things don't turn out as we had hoped.

It is also sensible to make sure that we have thought through our strategic options. We can start by identifying two or three strategies which might help us in achieving our ideal future. Having chosen potential options we can ask the following questions:

• What are the pros and cons of each option?

• What would be involved in each case?

• Do any of the strategic options or choices look clearly better than the others?

• Does our original vision still look reasonable and attainable?

If we believe it is worth progressing some options, we can also ask the question 'What if?' to explore how robust our strategies are likely to be in different circumstances. Here we can learn from the experience of an organisation like Shell, which develops scenarios that describe different environments. These are not necessarily the most likely possibilities, but they are plausible and consistent. The scenarios are then used to test the future vision and strategic objectives. How would strategies and plans be impacted in the different scenarios? What would the implications be?

Scenario-type thinking can be complemented by more conventional planning, where we start from the present situation and work forward.

- What is the critical path?

- Where are the crunch points likely to be?

- How can we keep our options open?

We can use programme and project management thinking to imagine and articulate all the various possibilities around a branched network extending into the future. The best routes can be found, and the impact of different decisions considered.

Once we test our thinking thoroughly, we should be in a position to refine our original vision and develop a more nuanced perspective. Different possibilities and opportunities emerge. We have a clearer idea of the best routes to follow. We are in a better position to take advantage of uncertainty.

CHAPTER 7

Exploring and
Experimenting

'All life is an experiment. The more experiments you make, the better.'

RALPH WALDO EMERSON

Feeling the way

Once we have decided what we want to achieve and in what direction we want to go, the next challenge is to make things happen.

In periods of stability, that can be relatively straightforward. For example, imagine you are unexpectedly promoted to a new management position in a successful, expanding company to oversee the building of new premises. You have the full support of your boss to go ahead with this exciting new project and real commitment from your colleagues. There is money available. You put a plan together, get it approved, and get it built. You keep a grip of the situation, and all goes to plan.

But imagine a different scenario. The company's financial situation unexpectedly deteriorates and money becomes tight, your boss leaves for another job, the weather delays things, the builder goes bankrupt, and the materials ordered don't arrive. In these circumstances, the challenge would not so much be 'driving things through regardless' as being agile and flexible enough to adjust the plans to fit the changing situation. The challenge would be either to find ways of achieving the original strategic objective or to refine the strategy – without losing support along the way.

In times of uncertainty, circumstances change in ways we cannot predict. We find that our original plans do not work exactly as we had expected. Sometimes resistance develops and it is trickier to get support. However, new opportunities may present themselves that we might be able to build on. We have the opportunity to explore different courses of action, talk with others, and test new ideas out to see what might work. We have to keep our options open, drop some of our original ideas, and come up with new ones.

Uncertainty dictates that standard solutions rarely work and we generally have to feel our way, step by step, towards a more customised solution that might fit our exact circumstances. It is a time for exploring and experimenting. The right approach emerges as the situation evolves. There is rarely one recipe for success. Compromises and trade-offs are inevitable. If we are prepared to be patient, stand back a little, and encourage behaviours which support our strategic objectives as they appear, we can often achieve our goals faster and with less energy and more commitment than if we try to force things through.

Looking for evidence

We may need to feel our way to the right answer, but not necessarily in the dark. It is only too easy to misjudge complex situations and jump to premature conclusions. If we fail to consider all the relevant information, we can get things badly wrong. Solutions are not always obvious or clear-cut.

Intuition and instinct are important but are limited by our personal experience, prejudices and perspectives. The true value of investing time and effort in 'checking the evidence' is that it allows us to challenge our own assumptions and beliefs. False beliefs are even more damaging than ignorance. As Mark Twain is purported to have said ' It aint what you don't know that gets you into trouble. It's what you know for sure that just aint so'.

Provided there is time, then, it makes sense in complex situations to get into the habit of reviewing the available data and not relying solely on common sense and experience. Professional pilots flying in good conditions can make visual assessments of where they are and how they are doing. But when they are flying at night or through cloud they are taught to rely on instruments – the evidence – rather than their instincts.

We came across an example of this with one of our clients – a large multinational organisation where there was a high turnover of young, talented engineers. The conventional wisdom was that this could be remedied by better induction, training, higher pay, and staged career progression. These solutions were put in place at considerable cost – but the engineers still kept on leaving. It was only when the evidence from employee survey data, turnover statistics and exit interviews was put together systematically that it became obvious that the real reason for people leaving was that there wasn't enough challenge in the job. People wanted more responsibility, not more support.

To get the most from an evidence-based approach, we need to be flexible enough to change our minds when new information becomes available. It is all too easy to fall into the trap of using new information and insights to corroborate our existing ideas, looking for evidence that supports these and discounting the facts that do not fit. This is called 'confirmation bias' and is something we are all subject to, particularly when we hold strong opinions on emotional issues.

We don't have to confine ourselves to learning from our own situation. We can also speed up the exploring phase by learning from what happens elsewhere, looking outwards at others' experiences and seeing what can be learned from 'best practice'. It's much easier to raise your own standards when you know how you compare with others and how they manage challenges. Even if we can't meet others face to face, there are now numerous online platforms that provide comparative data – though it's critical that we develop the capacity to differentiate between reliable and unreliable sources.

If it is so helpful to look externally, why do so many of us not do it? People can get so preoccupied with their own situations that they may not think of viewing things in context. They come to believe that their own circumstances are so unique, there is nothing they can learn from others. This is hardly ever the case. Behind this reluctance to learn from others may be a toxic combination of arrogance, a fear of finding out that others are 'better', or even laziness about checking out and keeping up to date with developments. Even if we decide to go our own way, it is always useful to know what others are doing and to make our decisions in light of the information we can gather.

Experimentation

The evidence-based approach we have just described aims to make sense of uncertainty by systematically gathering, analysing and reviewing data and information from previous experience in order to understand underlying principles, patterns and trends. It helps us anticipate what might happen in the future and to intervene, where appropriate, in an effort to shape the outcome on the basis of a deeper understanding of the overall system. This represents the classical 'gold standard' for dealing with uncertainty.

It is a fine approach, but it is unwise to rely on this alone. Collecting evidence is always retrospective, and what happened in the past may not be a reliable guide to the future, particularly when applied to complex systems where there are many unknowns, interactions, evolving circumstances, changing boundary conditions and emerging technology. And what happens if we do not have the time or resources to carry out all the research that is necessary? What can we do if we are faced with a unique, new and possibly fluid set of circumstances to which lessons from elsewhere are not immediately applicable?

Wherever feasible, it makes a lot of sense to experiment. Experimentation allows us to try out a number of possibilities 'in the moment' to see what works best. Let us take a simple example that many people face. Imagine that you move to a completely new city, either to study or to start a new job.

You have found a place to live, and you need to begin by rebuilding your life, developing a new network of friends, working out the best places to go and the best things to do with your time. You are excited about the new opportunities but are also feeling anxious about having to start afresh.

Of course, you can start off by researching thoroughly all the possibilities, but sooner or later you need to try things out.

Best not to over-commit and pay for a year's subscription to the local gym until you have seen it. Best not to get into a daily routine of going to one café if it turns out there are three more around the corner that are less expensive and have better coffee. Best to be wary of developing such a close friendship with the first person you meet that you don't have time to meet anyone else.

When we are in the experimentation phase, we need to make sure that we do not close down our options too quickly just because we want to reduce anxiety and get into a settled pattern. Change takes time. We need to have patience and the courage to take some risks if we are to be able to make the most of the new opportunities.

Resisting rushing

Indeed, a fundamental difficulty with the exploration and experimentation phase is that, initially, it increases uncertainty rather than reducing it. This is because, in this phase, our objective is to seek to understand our situation in more depth before acting. It is important to keep an open mind until the evidence comes in. We have to climb the Richmor Ridge first if we want to be able to get a view from the summit.

To do this means resisting the social pressure that is put on us by those who say they have our best interests at heart but who are actually driven by a desire to reduce their own anxiety. For people like this, immediate, decisive, speedy action is always the best way. A firm public commitment to one course of action is demanded; complete certainty and confidence is expected; actions should be driven through regardless of the circumstances; and changing one's mind is seen as a criminal offence.

We also need to resist the pressures that we put on ourselves. When there is a demand for quick results, it is enticing to believe that all we need to do is bring things to completion. There is a tendency then for us to think in the short term rather than the longer term. The temptation is to take immediate action, moving directly to implementation and adopting an impositional strategy. The risk with this approach though is that we may try and force through a generic, over-simplified solution which has not been properly researched and developed.

Let us take a hypothetical example. Imagine going to a doctor because you need to lose 10 kg weight. You have in-vestigated the best way to do this and have committed to a sensible programme of dietary change and exercise which will lose a steady 0.5 kg per week, so that after twenty weeks you will have reached your target. You will monitor your weight throughout and take appropriate corrective action – eating differently or adapting your exercise regime – if things don't seem to be going to plan. But how would you feel if the doctor were to respond to you by saying, 'That is all very well but as you cannot guarantee it and as it is better to get immediate results, I have decided to chop off your arms. It may hurt a bit, but you will get over it.' After the surgery, the doctor weighs you and points out that you have in fact lost 12 kg, even better than expected. Unfortunately, you are unable to shake her hand to thank her.

Organisations that focus exclusively on cutting costs often fall into this trap, slashing budgets without thinking through the consequences. Like chopping off their arms, this may get immediate results but rarely helps in the longer term. Short-term fixes make us feel better by reducing uncertainty – and can even look good at first sight – but in complex situations they rarely work. Real change takes time.

How can we avoid being seduced by the quick fix? Understanding and being in control of our emotions is key. It is important to be realistic about what it feels like to manage oneself through times of uncertainty. Periods of anxiety and doubt are to be expected.

Very often we ride an emotional rollercoaster, as explained in the diagram to follow. We start with high hopes and aspirations, but, as reality bites, we realise that things are not as straightforward as we thought. We may then go through a period when we struggle. Some days are exciting, others disappointing, and our confidence goes up and down. The important thing in these circumstances is that we are patient and persistent, and keep our cool.

Generally speaking, 'the struggle' is the most demanding phase to manage. If we let the inevitable frustrations get to us, we may become disillusioned and give up too soon. We may drive ourselves into a negative frame of mind and risk losing the support of people around us.

We know of one high-level leadership programme in a leading business school where the participants are deliberately

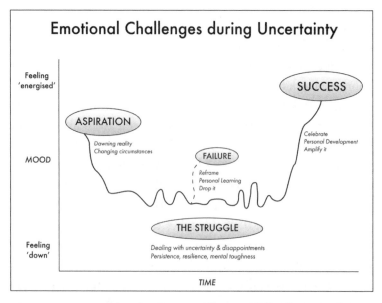

given a group task which is confusing, full of internal contradictions, vaguely explained, and impossible to do in the time allotted, as a way of simulating the 'struggle' phase. The participants are not told this until afterwards. The debrief is about how they coped with the frustration and disappointments – and how they managed relationships with their colleagues – rather than the outcome of the task. The intention of the task was to facilitate participants in developing necessary skills for life in a relatively safe environment.

Throughout 'the struggle' phase we have a choice as to whether to give up or persevere. Provided we make this choice on a rational basis, accepting 'failure' is not something to fear, and the choice that is made can result in an increase in positivity. Long-term success brings the most lasting rewards, but being prepared to 'let go' gives us the opportunity to learn, reframe our story, and start afresh. Failure is not something we should fear, but something we can learn from.

THE IMPORTANCE OF FAILURE

Companies involved in product design and innovation provide some great examples of the advantages of learning from 'failure'.

Take Sir James Dyson. The very first cyclone technology he and his mentor Jeremy Fry developed in the late 1970s took five years and numerous prototypes. Dyson explained that he made 5127 protoypes of his vacuum before he got it right. There were 5126 failures, but he learned from each one. He came to the conclusion that he didn't mind failure since that was how he had come up with a solution.

Dyson has institutionalised this approach, taking organisational learning to a systematic level. Recently, the company moved into a brand-new $200 million research facility. The mission of this facility is to 'experiment fearlessly, fail constantly and document those failures in company-issued black-and-yellow notebooks, which form the basis for still more experiments, still more failures.'

Trial and success

Experimentation does not always have to be a struggle. It can be an exhilarating experience in the right circumstances and if the conditions are set up in the right way.

'Trial and success' is a paradigm where the focus is on accentuating the positive and finding and backing winning approaches, rather than investing resources and effort in trying to change, block or stop less successful initiatives. It seeks to inspire rather than control, setting up conditions where creativity and innovation can flourish. Generally, the stage is set by explaining 'why', communicating the overall purpose, defining clear boundaries, setting targets, and encouraging people to develop new capabilities. This approach is particularly effective where people work together on a challenging activity which requires co-operation and teamwork. The emphasis is on involving and empowering people.

The case study below illustrates the characteristics of this approach. Experimentation works best in situations where people have some freedom, rather than in an environment where they are expected to follow orders. Trials should be small-scale, 'safe to fail' pilots, not ones that carry high risk. It is best to 'fail fast', so that the learning process is speeded up. And encouragement and social support can be very helpful.

TRIAL AND SUCCESS (Richard)

In May 2003 hundreds of business people embarked on the cruise ship Aurora at Southampton for a weekend of structured networking, business talks and entertainment. I was there as a guest speaker. After dropping off our bags in our cabins, our full group assembled in the main lecture theatre. None of us was sure what to expect – and we were surprised to find at each seat a simple percussion or wind musical instrument.

The unexpected continued. The presenter walked on to the stage and, without saying a word, managed to persuade one courageous person from the auditorium to stand up and make a noise with their instrument. He then encouraged others who had been given the same instrument to join in. He never spoke, but through a process of gestures, facial expressions and non-verbal encouragement eventually got a simple rhythm and tune established with this group. This process was then repeated with all the different types of instruments until every member of the audience was participating.

By this stage, it had dawned on everyone that the ultimate aim of this session was to learn to play a complex musical piece together. The audience dynamic was changing: people were beginning to improve and adjust their own playing without the need for much prompting from the presenter, even giving their own encouragement to the more talented among them. The presenter simply provided the overall orchestration, bringing together all the various components into a stirring finale, and keeping up the encouraging ethos.

It was all very musical. The sound was good. We were all delighted with ourselves and felt very motivated. And the co-ordinator still never said a word.

Building support

With a fun activity like the emergent orchestra, it's not difficult to keep people motivated and enthusiastic. But as we have seen, the exploration and experimentation phase can be challenging. It's during this phase that we try things out, knowing that not everything will be successful.

The uncertainty about success can make strong demands psychologically on our supporters. They can be taken on a rollercoaster ride, not really in control or knowing what is coming next. Not everything will work out as expected. But for any course of action to succeed, it helps if we have sufficient support to get over the inevitable bumps in the road.

In these circumstances, how can we keep them on board? There's no easy answer – but having a sure sense of purpose and values, communicating clearly, consistently and regularly, and adopting a positive, confident style can do wonders, particularly when people begin to see some early successes.

Over the longer haul, we need to be able to earn people's trust at a deep personal and emotional level. It is not just a question of having technical or professional credibility, but of earning trust as an individual and as a person. Once we have this, we are able to retain relationships through difficult circumstances, even during periods when we ourselves may not be at our best.

Building this level of trust takes time, effort and a degree of personal sacrifice. There is a considerable amount of research around this, and while the theory is relatively straightforward, putting it into practice is much harder. Some of the lessons that have been learned are as follows:

• Invest in communication. It is essential to make the time to meet people, explain what we are doing, and why. It is important to listen to them in ways which develop our understanding of what is happening and which builds both intellectual and emotional connection.

• Empathy is critical. We need to be sure we are connected and tuned in to 'the system' and understand where others are coming from.

• Be authentic. Levels of trust are re-evaluated with each inter-action that we have, so it is important to be consistent in our overall purpose and values and to come across as genuine. Our words and actions need to be congruent. It is important to be seen to stand our ground in the face of pressure.

• Show our supporters we are on their side and acting in their best interests. Likeability helps – for example through finding areas of common ground.

• Helping others without initially expecting a return also helps to build lasting relationships.

• Deliver. Keep our promises and provide evidence that we are making progress. Make the time to market and promote the story of what has been done.

• Make sure our external reputation and image aligns with our intentions.

Doing all this is far from easy. These are qualities that are familiar to public figures and those who have representational roles in public life, but they are not necessarily part of the everyday skills of the average person. They should be. There is nothing more helpful than the ability to develop relationships of trust and networks of support.

At the same time, we need to be realistic. In times of uncertainty and complexity we are highly unlikely ever to be in a position where everyone is on our side. The reality is that complex systems are inherently ambiguous and can be assessed differently by different people. Not everyone will agree with us, like us or trust us.

There are times when we must have the courage to act independently and go it alone.

CHAPTER 8

Acting Decisively

'I am waiting for the key people to support me on this issue,' said Terri.
'Should I come back next year then?' asked Richard.

The final countdown

Having found out what works on a small scale, the final stage in the Richmor Model is to implement our solution decisively and rapidly. *Carpe diem!*

Why this emphasis on speed? One way of looking at this is in terms of protecting our investment. In a volatile and fast-moving environment, the best solution that we have come up with during the 'exploration and experimenting' stage may soon be overtaken by events. If we don't pay sufficient attention to implementation, we can swiftly lose control of the situation. If we are too slow, we risk being managed by someone else in *their* interests rather than staying in control of our own destiny.

Dithering also allows time for any opponents to gather and potentially frustrate our plans. Small businesses are particularly vulnerable to this kind of scenario. Competitors do not stand still and may respond aggressively to change. The solutions that gain traction are those which get a foothold first and are backed by economies of scale. Some excellent ideas never see the light of day. Speed is of the essence.

Bold implementation also provides a great opportunity for us to communicate our 'story' in our own way, rather than letting others define it for us. This takes courage and there is always an element of risk, but if we have confidence in the work we have done so far, speedy implementation is not so much a leap of faith as a chance to change the landscape.

Who should be involved?

We may be able to take stock, strategise and explore situations on our own, but when it comes to taking action there are few situations where we are able to do things without some degree of support. Yet paradoxically our experience has been that 'acting decisively' is much more likely to be successful if at the early stages of planning and decision-making there are few rather than many people involved.

Conventional wisdom suggests that it is best to build a broad guiding coalition from the start if you want to effect change. In practice, however, we have found that the energy and time required to get a group together that genuinely agrees on complex issues and pays more than lip service to personal commitment from the outset is substantial.

Looking for full support at the early stages of implementation, especially where there is inherent uncertainty and risk, is unrealistic. Very often people will suspend judgement until they sense whether or not the initiative is likely to be a success. They may be busy on other matters anyway and will not initially want to spend too much time on it. Usually it is better to concentrate on keeping people informed about what is happening and making sure that the overall initiative is not blocked, rather than trying to persuade people to commit to extra work. Provided communication is consistent, and early results start to come in, people will sign up in their own time. The starting situation is unlikely to last for ever. People like to be part of a winning team!

Once we are clear on our decision-making process, we ought to be in a position to take action and get things under way. While we cannot delay too long, timing is critical. We have an opportunity to choose the time and place for what may be a battle ahead, and we need to do that wisely.

Are you ready?

From a strictly logical perspective, provided we have followed the steps in the Richmor Model we should be in a good position to move ahead. By the time we get to implementation, we should have a solution in mind which has a reasonable chance of working and which makes sense in the broader context.

It is not just logic that matters, though. There is psychological readiness to consider as well, particularly if the changes that are necessary affect us personally and demand that we act differently. Change requires us to give things up as well as embark on the new. There can be a strong temptation to stay with the status quo rather than commit to action, even at this point, as the reality of what we are about to embark on hits us.

We tend to be most committed to putting energy into change when we are not just intellectually convinced that it is the right thing to do but believe that making a change really matters. To quote an old adage: 'How many psychologists does it take to change a light bulb? Only one, but the light bulb really has to want to change!' If we genuinely feel a course of action is worthwhile and essential, then we are more likely to be committed to action. It is worth spending time thinking this through before proceeding further.

When other people are involved, the start of the implementation phase needs to be signposted, as it marks a different mindset from previous phases. We call this the 'no more dithery-doo' stage as 'focus' and 'action' predominate and the qualities of curiosity and inquiry are, for a period, relegated to the back burner. The experience of the explorer Sir Ernest Shackleton provides an excellent example of how the 'acting decisively' phase can be triggered.

PSYCHOLOGICAL READINESS: THE SHACKLETON *ENDURANCE* EXPEDITION

After nine months trapped in the Antarctic ice, including four months of winter darkness, Sir Ernest Shackleton the explorer carried out one last survey of his ship, the *Endurance*, at 5 p.m. local time on 27 October 1915.

He found the beams bending and snapping with a noise like heavy gunfire, and the decks breaking under his feet. In his memoir 'South', Shackleton writes about how he felt an overwhelming sense of relentless destruction as he saw what was happening.

Realising that the ship was being slowly crushed, there was now no hope of it being repaired, and with water flooding the lower decks, Shackleton turned to his crew of twenty-seven and gave the order to abandon ship, moving permanently onto the ice.

The journey home would now have to take place without the ship. With the exception of scientific photographs and a banjo, Shackleton instructed each crew member to dump all but 2 lbs of their personal possessions, as they began a new life on the ice, in the newly constructed Ocean Camp. Some 120 of 500 precious glass plates were rescued. The rest were smashed to avoid the temptation to return later and risk life attempting to save them.

Of course, it helps to have an implementation plan. At this stage, this does not need to be a detailed project listing with every 'i' dotted and 't' crossed, but rather an overall strategic framework which provides for some flexibility and allows for more detailed plans to be developed as the situation unfolds. Typically this plan should include:

• Ensuring the 'why' has been thought through and a broad picture can be painted of the reasons for the change and the intended outcome. This should be tested from the perspective of all those whose support is needed for success.

• Clarifying 'how' the change is to be implemented, focusing on the process, decision-making, communication and style rather than detailed content.

• Setting challenging targets and deadlines which are relatively short-term (generally less than three months), specific, and intended to be made public.

Keeping things moving

Decisive action tends to draw in more people as it progresses. Once the decision to take action has been made, it is not magic that is needed to keep things moving, but good leadership. In our case study example, we described how Sir Ernest Shackleton made the tough decision to abandon the *Endurance* after it had become stuck in the ice in the course of his failed Antarctic expedition. The continuing story of how he eventually managed to lead all his men to safety provides a classic lesson in excellent leadership. Somehow, in the most difficult of circumstances, Shackleton was able to create a sense of optimism, shared purpose, and unity in his team, and a commitment to what was initially an unwelcome course of action.

A large part of this was down to Shackleton's personal qualities. He was an excellent role model, always putting the needs of the team above his own and providing an example of respect, resilience and calmness in times of extreme uncertainty. He made detailed plans, but was flexible enough to change them if and when the situation demanded. He kept his finger on the pulse of what was going on at all times.

Back in the everyday world, our experience has been that courage, determination and keeping your nerve – not flinching at the last minute – still matter. Self-discipline is a must. Resisting inappropriate social pressure, for example not being seduced by flattery or driven off-course by bullying, is critical. Knowing how and when to use power and negotiation to keep things moving without damaging the social fabric is important too, while we also have to ensure that we have the right organisation and resources in place and that people know what is expected of them.

Drawing on established change management theory and practice, for example the models of organisational change developed by the Harvard professor John Kotter, can be very helpful at this stage. Some key factors are:

• Pay attention to identifying and removing barriers to change.

• Systematically analyse and resolve problems.

• Monitor and communicate progress.

• Reward and recognise those who contribute.

• Ensure there is continued support.

• Continually build capability to deal with challenges.

It is important to make sure we do not get so wrapped up in operational duties – getting our tasks done – that we forget to invest the time and effort necessary to keep people on board. One way of avoiding this is to routinely carry out a systematic analysis of stakeholders, identifying all those who are impacted by our plans and/or whose contribution is necessary for success. Once we have done this, we are in a position to assess how much power and influence they have and how supportive they are. We can then come up with a plan for doing something about it. Sometimes it is only when we do a systematic analysis like this that we realise there are people with whom we have not engaged properly and who may be blocking change.

When projects have a wide scope, developing a support network that can lend a hand if things get tricky or when they grow rapidly in scale can pay dividends in the long run. These are people from a variety of backgrounds who are likely to be supportive of the overall concept, enthusiastic about helping, and credible. The key is to develop, from the start, a network of people who are on our side. Social media makes it possible to reach large numbers of people and build bands of followers in this way, and this makes it much easier to scale up and disseminate ideas quickly when the time comes.

Focus on data

Paying attention to the facts and data can make a big difference in helping us to focus our attention on the specific things we need to address. We have to be careful that our desire to foster 'decisive action' and maintain the pace does not result in our enthusiasm overriding our judgement. It is important that 'keeping things moving' doesn't deteriorate into trying to force things through because we are in a rush.

A logical and pragmatic approach to problem resolution is likely to yield much better results than using power as a blunt instrument. It is important to keep things as simple as possible and to use data to help us be realistic about what is in our control and what is not – as the following case study shows.

THE ART OF THE POSSIBLE (Richard)

Early in my career, I worked as a management consultant for a bus company. I was assigned to work at a bus garage in south London to help them improve the availability of buses. At the time, over 100 buses out of the 500 based there were off the road awaiting maintenance, resulting in waiting times of up to forty minutes. I was told the situation was hopeless. The problem was that new buses had been introduced and their gearboxes kept breaking down unpredictably in the heavy London traffic. This was outside the garage's control.

Working with the garage manager, I conducted an informal review of the various other managers and supervisors across the district to see what we could learn

---

from best practice. It turned out there was a strong correlation between the volume of the supervisor's voice and their performance. The loudest, most autocratic team leaders were the most effective in getting spare parts. We called this 'management by decibels'.

We were stuck. Both the failure of gearboxes and the dysfunctional 'spares' system were outside the garage's control, and training supervisors to speak more loudly and bully others was neither an attractive nor a sustainable option. So we turned our attention to the immediate problem which was under the garage's control – clearing the backlog. We calculated how many extra maintenance staff were needed, given the average rate of failure. The maths showed that if two additional staff were redeployed to this activity, the backlog would be fixed in four months. The garage manager implemented this approach despite strong opposition from those around him. It took courage to find a way of redeploying existing staff. He was also able to put in a regular order for gearboxes rather than waiting until a bus broke down. Performance monitoring was introduced and targets openly displayed.

Within four months, there were less than five buses waiting for maintenance, and waiting times were a thing of the past. We had become the 'best practice' garage.

Focusing on what we could do something about rather than what we could not brought results. And logic and reason turned out to be more helpful than 'management by decibels'.

Consolidating gains

Once we have been successful in putting into effect our chosen solution, there is generally still work to do to ensure that it 'sticks'. It takes time and effort to learn new behaviours and skills – and very often a lot of practice. It can be tempting to give up when the initial novelty wears off. Not only that, but when the going gets tough there is a tendency to revert to old patterns of behaviour and the status quo.

Let us take a simple example. Imagine someone has decided to make a concerted effort to get fit. They conclude that it would be sensible to go to the gym each morning rather than watch breakfast TV in bed. It is hard at first, but soon they get into a new routine and begin to feel much healthier. All works well until they go on holiday and arrive back jet-lagged. Too tired to go to the gym, they stay at home. This pattern continues the next day, and the day after – and soon they find themselves back at square one.

At a psychological level, this comes down to habit. Over a period of time our brains learn to respond to specific cues by converting complex series of actions into automatic routines – habits – which we do not have to think about and which take little effort. The alarm wakes us up and we turn the TV on to watch the morning news. If we are sufficiently determined to make a change, we can learn to replace one habit with another, which becomes the new habit. The alarm rings and we go to the gym.

To consolidate even a simple change like this requires a systematic effort. A combination of measures might be needed, for example the following:

• Ensure continued buy-in to the reasons for change (buy scales to monitor weight).

• Get rid of the original triggers (remove TV from bedroom).

• Ensure the new routine is as easy as possible (pack gym kit the night before).

• Ensure that new behaviours are rewarded (watch TV while exercising at gym and enjoy subsequent high-quality shower).

• Develop a social support network (get to know others at gym who regularly use the same slot).

When it comes to consolidating complex change, especially in organisations, the social dynamics are particularly important. It helps if everyone involved is recognised and rewarded for doing things in the new way rather than rewarded for the old status quo. This avoids what has been termed 'the folly of rewarding A while expecting B'. Unfortunately, changes to the reward system often lag behind changes in expectations.

It is also important to ensure sufficient attention is paid to spreading the word and communicating success. Once something is well known, it can be a lot more difficult to dislodge. Social media, video, TED talks, conference presentations, public seminars and magazine articles can all form part of an integrated communication strategy – as can a willingness to take part in best practice exchanges. We have found that asking people who have been trained as part of a support network to act as ambassadors has helped to reinforce new ways of doing things.

Indeed, a spirit of magnanimity and inclusion makes it a lot easier to sustain changes in organisations. Involving people and spreading the credit for success can help build a solid group who have self-interest in consolidating the gains. It helps build social capital and engender support the next time round. It is also often worthwhile to make the effort to reconcile with those who were originally opposed to change. This was a strategy used to great effect by Nelson Mandela which enabled him to build high levels of support for successive initiatives. Maintaining quality relationships with opponents as well as supporters can be important in the long term.

If we are successful in putting all this into place, we may find ourselves back where we started, in a situation of relative certainty and comfort. The change has become the new status quo. Perhaps we may even begin to feel stuck once more. Could it be time to think about starting the Richmor process again?

CHAPTER 9

Making the Most
of Uncertainty

'Should we keep to the beaten track?' asked Richard.
'Why not try a different way?' suggested Terri.
'That could be more interesting.'

THE ROAD LESS TRAVELLED (Terri)

Some years ago, I rented a house on the east coast of Ireland just outside Dublin city. The area had a four-mile-long beach with sand dunes. Many mornings I went for an early-morning walk on the beach.

Initially, I followed the well-worn track on the dunes which led to the beach. One morning I thought, 'Why am I following this track laid down by previous walkers? What if I started a track of my own?'

The first morning was tricky. The marram grass was prickly, and I was attacked by sharp spikes. The next morning, I sought out my route of the previous day. It was hard to find. With a bit of effort, though, I found it again and after a week of walking it I could see the beginnings of a new track.

After two weeks a new pathway had been laid down. Persisting with my exploration had created a new way. Not only did this become my preferred route, but others tried to use it also.

Time for a reset?

A feeling of being stuck applies to many of us at one time or another in our lives. Even if we are naturally adventurous, have a positive outlook, welcome a challenge, and enjoy variety, novelty and change, there are bound to be times when we feel that our lives have become routine.

Very often, the underlying problem is that without really intending to, we become creatures of habit, preferring stability and structure to challenge and change. We get into routines which for the most part serve us well. We go to the same places, and meet the same people in those same places at the same times each day. We get our news from the same sources. We live in the same location. We become part of a community which shares similar ideas and values. Our lives are ordered and busy. We go on holidays from time to time to have a break and then 'come back to reality'.

We become so focused on just getting on with our lives that we do not invest much time or effort in thinking about why we are doing what we are doing – and what the future might hold. Perhaps we are a little scared of doing that. Even when we do think ahead, we may make detailed plans on the assumption that things will continue in much the same, pre-dictable way. After all, if we are fairly content with our lives, why change them?

• Why invest time and energy in making unnecessary changes?

• Why make ourselves anxious by worrying about things outside our control?

- Is it not best to ensure things remain as they are?

- Why think too much?

- Why not just get on with things?

The value of uncertainty is that it can present us with a host of opportunities to break these patterns and ultimately lead a more fulfilling life. Rather than waiting for the inevitable crisis to occur and finding that we are forced to change, it is possible to use the variability and inherent opportunities associated with uncertainty to create our own path. We can make our own choices. We don't have to squander our time waiting for things to settle back to an illusory normality. We can consider if it is time for a reset.

Ditching defensiveness

It is easy to see how we can become set in our ways. Our default mindset for dealing with uncertainty is usually a defensive one. When we are in a defensive mode our priority becomes one of self-protection, stress reduction and keeping workload and effort to a minimum. We focus on the short term and what is in our immediate self-interest.

To do this we shield ourselves from the outside world, accepting that most of what is happening is simply beyond our control. We actively seek to block new unpalatable information, carrying on regardless and battening down the hatches. This is illustrated in the diagram which follows.

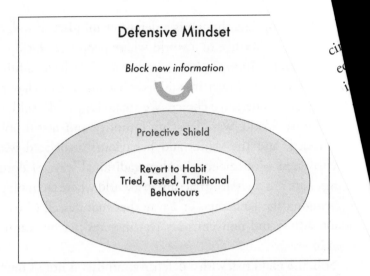

In the short term, a defensive mindset can be much less stressful and less demanding on us personally. It allows us to reassure ourselves that all is well and that we don't have to worry too much, so minimising anxiety. We focus on coping rather than looking for opportunity. We consider that our personal responsibility for shaping events is limited, and we protect ourselves from the outside world.

Where we are genuinely powerless to do anything to change things, faced with outside forces that are either uncontrollable or just too chaotic for us to comprehend, a defensive mindset makes sense. For example, soldiers fighting in the trenches in the First World War were faced with the most awful circumstances. They had little choice but to obey orders, their environment was both dangerous and unpleasant, and they had no idea whether they would live or die. Yet they possessed a camaraderie, stoicism and sense of humour which helped them through these dreadful times. They found ways of shielding themselves from reality.

How appropriate though is a defensive mindset in today's circumstances? We live in a world where people are far more educated and informed than ever before. We have infinite information at our fingertips and have become used to having a high degree of personal choice. We are no longer like soldiers in the First World War. Trust in authority and institutions has eroded, and the values and behaviours associated with defensiveness – obedience, loyalty, traditional ways of doing things – are not obviously relevant in a world where technology is changing the landscape in a way that requires all of us to adapt, adjust and reinvent ourselves in ways that we cannot even foresee.

Still, the main risk with a defensive mindset is not so much that it is no longer a close fit with today's circumstances but that it just will not work. Putting one's head in the sand in a rapidly changing world is a huge gamble. Being unaware of or in denial of changing realities can be harmful for our physical health, psychological well-being and personal effectiveness. As time goes by, the inadequacy of simply keeping to our traditional ways becomes more obvious. What we have done in the past is no longer appropriate. For example, not keeping up with new technology can result in our being deskilled and feeling left behind. Once we feel we are under threat, there is the temptation to alleviate anxiety through self-medication, over-indulgence or angry outbursts at others.

Pursuing proactivity

In an uncertain world, we believe a proactive mindset based on the Richmor Model is superior in principle to the protective approach we have just described. Rather than trying to pretend uncertainty does not exist, it ultimately makes more sense to use uncertainty as a catalyst for change, doing things differently and undertaking personal reinvention.

Whereas in a protective approach the focus is external, *shielding* ourselves from anxiety and stress, the emphasis with a proactive mindset is on *developing* ourselves. It requires openness, a learning mindset, and curiosity. Rather than defend ourselves with a rigid protective shield that blocks all new information, we remain flexible and open to the outside world and proactively manage the information we receive so that we do not get overloaded with data or overwhelmed with anxiety. We look for opportunities and try to find out, pragmatically, what works and what does not work.

We use this proactive approach together with our personal sense of purpose to explore and try to shape our environment. We rely on a strong core – our character, ethics and personal values – to keep us functioning effectively. All this is illustrated in the diagram below.

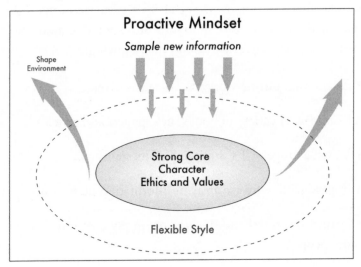

137

Cutting out unnecessary data that does not add value is an essential part of this proactive approach. There is an immense amount of information available and we have only so much capacity to interpret it. For example, faced with a constant barrage of bad news from twenty-four-hour media, there is a case to be made for rationing how much of it we listen to. Why waste time on things we cannot influence, that make us miserable? This is a strategy that a number of high-profile politicians have apparently adopted. Former British prime minister Theresa May reportedly cut out reading the morning newspapers during Brexit negotiations for these very reasons, relying on a summary instead.

Of course, with any strategy to manage information, it is important that the sampling system we deploy limits the quantity of information we take in but does not result in our receiving only information that we want to hear. For a proactive approach to work, we need to listen to a wide range of opinions, views and perspectives rather than people with similar views to our own. Social media can accentuate this state of affairs. To be certain that we are exposed to a variety of ideas and perspectives we can do the following:

- Ensure that our network of contacts is diverse.

- Read a wide variety of books, newspapers and articles.

- Watch a range of TV stations and programmes.

- Engage with a diverse array of information platforms.

- Learn from travel and the arts, or simply chat informally to more people.

All these activities will help to broaden our perspective.

A proactive mindset is also greatly facilitated by a supportive culture. Genuine proactivity is unlikely to be practical in circumstances where people have limited freedom, have little discretion in how they can organise their lives, or have no choice in how they speak, act or behave because of religious, political or cultural oppression. Their challenges are initially likely to be more social and political than psychological or personal. Having said that, our experience has been that there can be a great appetite for proactive thinking as these kinds of societies develop.

Those who have a preference for authoritarianism and 'strong leadership' may not find a proactive approach immediately appealing. According to the American psychologist Jeffrey Saltzman, the 'authoritarian personality' was first explored as a concept at the end of the Second World War and was defined as 'a desire for security, order, power, and status, with a desire for structured lines of authority, a conventional set of values or outlook, a demand for unquestioning obedience, and a tendency to be hostile toward or use as scapegoats individuals of minority or non-traditional groups'.

Recent research by political scientist Matthew MacWilliams suggests that a substantial minority of Americans (16–30 per cent) currently have a preference for authoritarianism and that this proportion increases if people feel under threat. This may well be true in other societies.

On the other hand, a proactive approach is not the preserve of a 'cosmopolitan liberal elite'. Having a strong core and personal values is arguably as important for success as possessing intellectual firepower. David Goodhart, British journalist and author, describes how our societies have become increasingly divided into two rival value blocks: the 'anywheres' and 'somewheres'. 'Anywheres' have identities based on educational and career success, allowing them to be generally comfortable and confident with new places and people. They value autonomy, fluidity and openness. 'Somewheres' have more specific identities – Scottish farmer, American miner from Pittsburgh – based on group belonging and particular places. The 'somewheres' are more rooted – they value familiarity and security – and this plays a part in their development of value systems.

Proactivity makes strong demands on people. At the heart of the proactive approach is a willingness to be open to experience and to have a tolerance for ambiguity. There is a need for balance, maturity and personal judgement, as well as the intellectual capacity to think for ourselves. We need to be clear on 'who we are' and 'what we stand for', combining a strong core set of ethics and values with a flexibility of style that enables us to connect with and relate to a wide variety of people.

We have to achieve this tricky balance in a way that other people see as authentic, which is quite a challenge in a world where our every interaction can be recorded and broadcast to the masses via social media and may be decontextualised or misconstrued in the process. We also have to remain open to changing some of our core attitudes and beliefs if evidence emerges that we have been wrong or that these beliefs are no longer appropriate.

Despite these caveats and challenges, there is a strong case for encouraging more people to think proactively. Whatever the difficulties, it is more likely to work.

Making proactivity a habit

How can we make proactivity a habit? We have talked about how the Richmor Model can be used to deal with major episodes of uncertainty as they come along, but can it also be used proactively in a systematic, routine way for dealing with smaller, everyday challenges? If so, this can help us to make the most of uncertainty.

In order to do this, the four Richmor Steps are simply positioned as elements of a continuous 'learning cycle', as shown in the diagram below.

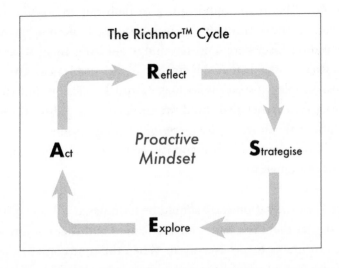

The Richmor™ Cycle

Reflect

Proactive Mindset

Act

Strategise

Explore

Reflect The first stage of the cycle is to take stock, reflect on how things are going, and decide whether or not it is time to consider a change of course. It is important that we are balanced, objective and not overly self-critical – paying attention to our 'successes' as well as any 'failures' – so that we develop a positive, learning mindset. We can then ask and answer the following two questions: 'Given all this, can I still achieve my original objectives? Might I need to do something differently?'

Strategise If we do need to think about doing things differently, the next step is to reassess our overall vision and purpose and develop a number of possible options which are consistent with these as well as being within our control. There is no point in wasting time and energy on things that we cannot influence.

Explore This is the opportunity to flesh out the options in detail, to think through the implications, look at what has been done elsewhere, and try things out on a small scale to see what works. It is at this stage that patience is necessary, as most people's instinct is to make a quick decision and rush into action rather than hold fire until there is greater clarity. In uncertain times, *if time permits*, keeping options open can be a wise course of action and can result in better customised solutions emerging.

Act The exploration stage should be terminated as soon as it is clear that there is a best course of action and that conditions are favourable for its execution. When the time comes to act, it is important to move fast and implement decisively.

Thinking in this way helps us to continually review and update our options when we are in a changing environment. We see this approach as complementary to Deming's PDCA (**P**lan, **D**o, **C**heck, **A**ct) cycle, which is an iterative four-step management method that is used extensively in quality management, generally in relatively stable environments. The RSEA cycle (**R**eflect, **S**trategise, **E**xplore, **A**ct) is consistent with this but has the broader perspective that is needed in uncertain circumstances, when there are not only *logical decisions* to be made based on the facts but *strategic choices* to be made based on values and purpose as well as data.

Over time, this way of thinking can become so automatic that no special arrangements are required, and the principles of RSEA can be used to make choices on the best course of action even in fast-moving crisis situations where speed is critical.

PROACTIVITY IN A CRISIS SITUATION

Chesley Sullenberger and Jeff Skiles, the pilots who safely ditched their plane in the Hudson River in New York in 2009 following a bird strike and engine failure, implicitly followed an 'RSEA' type approach in making the decision to land in the river rather than return to an airport. The entire process took a matter of minutes.

Following the bird strike, they realised quickly that both engines had lost power and were unable to be re-started. In conjunction with ground staff, they initially examined options of returning to LaGuardia airport or diverting to nearby Teterboro airport.

They explored these very quickly, taking into account their previous experience, the exact circumstances, and the relevant protocols, before reaching the conclusion that neither of these options was likely to work. They realised that in fact the best option would be to bring the plane down on the Hudson River and they then acted decisively to achieve this. In doing so, many lives were saved.

Subsequent official reviews and simulations have confirmed that their response was appropriate given the situation they were in.

People who make a habit of thinking proactively can sometimes run the risk of being misunderstood. Of course, they have the capacity to be as strong and decisive as anyone else once the evidence is clear. But the fact that they are open-minded, enthusiastic about exploring different options, and prepared to adapt their starting position pragmatically when they find what works leaves them open to criticism and accusations of inconsistency, particularly if those around them crave a higher level of certainty.

Sometimes these perceptions are valid, sometimes not. Each part of the cycle brings its own issues.

• 'Reflect' behaviours can be interpreted as lacking commitment, wasting time, not backing the system, or showing doubt.

• 'Strategising' can be characterised as pie in the sky, unrealistic or displaying personal ambition.

• 'Exploring' can be interpreted as unable to decide, slow or unfocused.

• 'Act' behaviours can be seen as ruthless, not listening, and driven by power.

The way to address these perceptions is by being authentic and making sure that one's core purpose, values and ethics are clear, consistent and communicated well. Indeed, the biggest challenges with putting the Richmor approach into practice are associated with developing the attitudes, mindset and skills needed to make it work.

These are covered in more detail in the next chapter.

CHAPTER 10
Developing Competencies

*'Thinking is the hardest work there is, which is probably
the reason why so few engage in it.'*

HENRY FORD

The starting point

To recap on the challenge of dealing with uncertainty, we know that it requires many psychological skills such as intuition, logic, resilience and self-awareness. If we are to do it well, we must take personal responsibility, take risks, and be able to keep things in perspective. It requires both consistency and flexibility.

We also know that a proactive approach to uncertainty makes greater demands on people than a defensive strategy. It is not as simple or straightforward. It can be more emotionally demanding, it takes more effort, and there is less shared societal experience of what is involved. Consider, for example, the demands at each stage of the Richmor Cycle as outlined below:

Reflect: Finding the space and time to reflect, understanding the external environment and assessing how it is changing – requiring critical thinking skills to evaluate strengths and weaknesses, objectivity, realism, and the capacity to manage emotions including anxiety;

Strategise: Developing a vision and strategic options for the future – requiring a broad perspective, imagination, creativity, analytical skills and courage;

Explore: Evaluating and testing the various options – requiring research and evaluation competencies, social skills (networking, influencing, collaborating), and personal skills including patience;

Act: Implementing ideas and getting things done – requiring confidence, resilience, communication, change management skills and self-discipline.

As well as these 'process competencies' directly related to this RSEA cycle, there are also a number of professional, technical and personal competencies which can help: for example, a facility for social media and communication, presentation skills, and analytical problem-solving. Subject matter expertise can also be important. If faced with uncertainty about the best way forward for a business, having some knowledge of the sector is a definite bonus.

Most importantly, broad conceptual, personal, and relationship competencies are required for a proactive approach to work. We have to use the whole range of our abilities in a coherent and integrated way. Skills in thinking, managing relationships and managing oneself are combined for a common purpose. These are the qualities of personal leadership which provide the main focus for this chapter. While they can develop naturally as a result of experience, the process can be accelerated by structured and targeted development.

Role models for uncertainty

Some people are naturally more comfortable dealing with uncertain situations than others. Our experience has been that those who 'get it' can be of quite varied backgrounds, age and ability but share a common desire to make a difference. They have a strong sense of personal responsibility, are interested not just in themselves but in the bigger picture, and have the ability to get on well with people. They tend to be psychologically mature, balanced, and have strong personal values.

Personality, education and cultural background also play a part. Someone who is open to experience and learning, is psychologically stable, well-educated, and from a society which encourages challenge starts at a different end of the spectrum from an anxious person who lacks confidence, fears change, and is part of an organisation, society or broader system that discourages people from thinking too much for themselves.

On the global stage, the person who stands out as being extraordinarily capable of dealing with uncertainty is the late President of the Republic of South Africa, Nelson Mandela. He had the boldest and most challenging of visions – to bring apartheid to an end – and he was ultimately hugely successful on both a political and personal level. During his life, he had to deal with years of uncertainty, intimidation, violence and personal risk.

We had the privilege of visiting his home in Soweto when running a course on human resources management in Johannesburg, South Africa. What did we learn about him?

CASE STUDY ON PERSONAL LEADERSHIP AND UNCERTAINTY
(Nelson Mandela)

During his life, Nelson Mandela was faced with long periods of uncertainty yet he was able to adjust and adapt to these, demonstrating high levels of personal leadership. The spirit that enabled Mandela to succeed was rooted in the abilities and competencies he demonstrated in a number of areas:

• He was able **to see the big picture**, realising that apartheid was not a viable, ethical or acceptable solution for South Africa. He was brave enough to tackle this issue, maintained a long-term perspective, and could be objective and tough-minded where necessary.

• He was able **to build relationships and support**, earning respect from people at all levels of society, even those who were his enemies. He demonstrated empathy, understanding and the ability to communicate with others regardless of their background. He sought to find the 'middle way' where possible and showed compassion and forgiveness when required.

• He had the ability **to manage himself**, showing courage in the face of adversity and being willing to accept a degree of personal risk. Even under pressure and threat, for example during his trial, he demonstrated a steadfast adherence to his personal values. He showed resilience, mental and physical toughness in surviving over twenty-five years in prison, and perseverance and patience in reaching his goals.

• He had a **strong character**, driven by beliefs rather than personal gain.

The Richmor competencies

We have summarised key competencies that support a proactive approach to uncertainty using a model based on the Irish shamrock, with three leaves and a core stem. The framework is consistent with the personal leadership qualities exhibited by Nelson Mandela as outlined above and other notable inspirational figures.

The shamrock is a living organism. While it occurs naturally, it can be grown and cultivated. It can be harvested, spreads widely, and has acquired an iconic, symbolic status reflective of a deeper meaning. It is also associated with good fortune. All in all, it provides an interesting basis for thinking about leadership.

These different elements reflect the skills needed to navigate through turbulent times. The three leaves of the plant represent the intellectual, interpersonal and self-management competencies which we deem to be important if people are to be as effective as possible in an uncertain environment. These are connected and rooted through a fourth element, the stem of the plant. This provides a metaphor for how a person's core character, purpose and values are an integrating and supportive element for the different competencies.

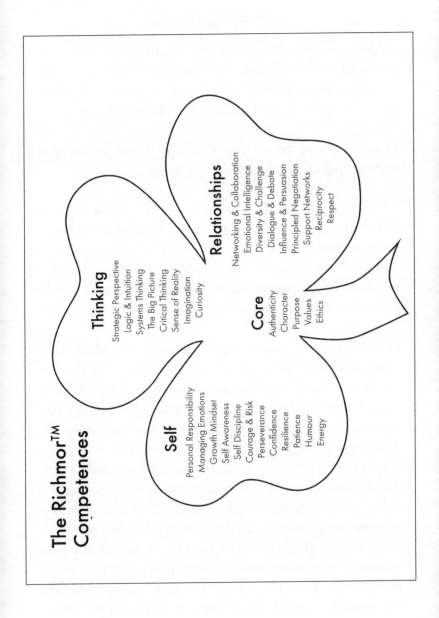

The Richmor™ Competences

Thinking

Strategic Perspective
Logic & Intuition
Systems Thinking
The Big Picture
Critical Thinking
Sense of Reality
Imagination
Curiosity

Relationships

Networking & Collaboration
Emotional Intelligence
Diversity & Challenge
Dialogue & Debate
Influence & Persuasion
Principled Negotiation
Support Networks
Reciprocity
Respect

Core

Authenticity
Character
Purpose
Values
Ethics

Self

Personal Responsibility
Managing Emotions
Growth Mindset
Self Awareness
Self Discipline
Courage & Risk
Perseverance
Confidence
Resilience
Patience
Humour
Energy

Developing thinking

Dealing more proactively with uncertainty makes strong demands on intellectual skills. At all stages of the Richmor Cycle there is a need for people to think more for themselves, which generally requires a combination of intuition and logic.

• Curiosity, imagination and a sense of reality are blended together in painting a picture of the future.

• Critical thinking is used to explore and evaluate options, and analytical skills and a strong sense of reality are necessary in the implementation phase.

• A sense of perspective, objectivity and a systems thinking orientation is necessary throughout.

How can these qualities and skills be developed? Ideally they should be encouraged from an early age, as we know that the first two to three years of life have an enormous impact. These skills should then be nurtured and developed further through the education system. Unfortunately, in too many cases this does not happen. Learning to pass examinations with a high grade can take priority over encouraging curiosity and inquiry. Standardised objective assessments are often given excessive attention. Those who attend a third-level college may have more opportunities to learn the necessary thinking skills.

So it is not always possible to rely on the formal education system. Fortunately, however, 'thinking' is a skill that people can develop at any life stage if the desire and opportunities are available, through a combination of further education, training, coaching and practical experience gained by assignments and facilitated experiential learning.

Broadening one's experience is a good way to start. People can end up with a rather narrow view of the world if they become too focused on the here and now. 'Bringing the outside in' by visiting other places, searching for best practice, and talking to people who have already had similar experiences can be valuable. Learning gained from art, literature, travel, theatre and sport can provide useful insights into creative thinking. In our work with organisations we have used music and painting as ways of encouraging senior managers to use their intuition more when considering the future.

Understanding the context in which we are operating makes it easier for us to contribute and speak up. When we work with organisations, we sometimes introduce regular 'strategy' sessions which provide people with the opportunity to learn more about what is happening to their business and their environment. In organisational terms it can help to be able to see ourselves as 'actors in a play' rather than interpreting everything from a self-centred perspective.

When dealing with complex issues it's important to:

• Take a step back and challenge assumptions rather than feel pressurised to come up with a quick solution.

• Find the right questions to ask and make sure that the problem is properly defined before rushing to 'the answer' .

• Invest upfront in clarifying the 'why' and the 'what' rather than going straight to the 'how'.

• Make sure that the challenge is well articulated and described in systems terms rather than just focusing on one aspect.

It is especially important to develop critical thinking capabilities in a world where we are bombarded with information from so many sources, much of which is unverified and some of which inevitably involves educated guesswork about an unpredictable future. It is hard to know what is true and what is not. There are psychological factors at work here.

• Do we feel we are under threat, or powerless to change things?

• Do we feel we are in control?

• Do we personally trust the source of the data?

In these situations, it is all too easy to end up with a 'trust no one' mentality, where we are especially sceptical of information from 'experts' and those in authority, because we doubt their motives and question their capabilities. We may waste our time inventing conspiracy theories to explain what we imagine are their motivations, rather than looking rationally at what they are actually saying, critically examining it, and using this to move our own thinking forward. Once we are in a defensive mode, our lack of trust means that we are more susceptible to listening only to what we want to hear, and this leaves us vulnerable to manipulation by others, to propaganda, and to fake news.

Better education and specific training on critical thinking can help in this respect, but the underlying psychological issues must also be addressed. The key to improving critical thinking is for people to feel they are personally in control.

There are common thinking traps which are best avoided when dealing with complex systems, including the following:

• Generalisation occurs when broad universal beliefs are formed on the basis of a few facts.

• Polarisation and rigid thinking divide issues into black and white polarities so that people feel they have no choices beyond these extremes.

• Catastrophising is a mindset that assumes that regardless of what decisions are made they are likely to end in disaster.

Challenging these assumptions and encouraging people to test their thinking through checking the evidence results in a more pragmatic and less dogmatic approach. It helps people understand what is really in their control and what is not, and helps them to develop a clearer understanding of the implications of their choices.

Mastering ourselves

To master uncertainty, we have to learn to master ourselves. Fundamental to that is learning to manage our own emotions, especially anxiety. A whole industry has developed around this, with well-documented tools and techniques including meditation and mindfulness, as well as recommendations on exercise, diet and sleep. Cognitive behavioural therapy (CBT) is regarded as particularly effective in helping people manage anxiety and control their irrational fears.

Building self-awareness is important for development. What is the best way to achieve this? To some extent the growth of self-awareness happens naturally: as we age, we generally become more aware of what we can and cannot do, what we like and what we do not like. The challenge is how to speed this process up so we do not have to wait a lifetime to gain wisdom.

There are many ways to do this. There are those who value a scientific approach and the insights gained through psycho-metric tests, generally requiring the completion of a structured questionnaire through self-assessment. This can be augmented with observations by others to provide a more objective per-spective. In organisations, assessments by a person's manager, subordinates and peers are sometimes combined with self-assessment in '360-degree' feedback.

However, the most straightforward way of gaining insight is simply to encourage people around us to give us honest feedback – and listen to it. This is not as easy as it sounds. Honest feedback can be hard to deal with when we first receive it, especially if it dents our self-image. And sometimes people are reluctant to tell us the truth for fear we might be offended, or that it might turn us against them. Consequently, honest feedback is invaluable for those in positions of power. Both Eleanor Roosevelt and Clementine Churchill, for example, provided feedback to their partners which kept them grounded.

Another way of improving self-awareness is by observing non-judgementally our own manner of thinking and feeling through the practice of mindfulness or meditation. There are those who argue that since our inner life and experience is only directly accessible to ourselves, this represents the purest form of self-awareness. This approach may also have other benefits in improving our sense of well-being.

'Vertical development', which involves developing people to think in more complex, strategic, systemic and interdependent ways, is just as important as horizontal development, which is the acquisition of specific skills and knowledge. Ultimately this is characterised by interdependent, collaborative, longer-term thinking. People who have reached a high level of development are able to see systems, patterns and connections, can look at things from different angles, and can manage ambiguity and contradictions. In the first stage of vertical development, people typically move from seeking direction and relying on authority to being much more self-directed, independent thinkers, motivated by achievement and driven by their internal compass. To encourage this, it is important that high-potential people are not mollycoddled early in their career and that leadership development programmes are not over-organised. Spoon-feeding people does not prepare them for real-world challenges.

If building self-awareness is the starting point, taking personal responsibility and ownership for ourselves, rather than blaming others, is the next step in developing a proactive approach. Usually this means we need the courage to take some risks and move away from our comfort zone. As the playwright Neil Simon pointed out, if no one ever took risks, Michelangelo would have painted the Sistine floor.

Understanding our own attitudes to risk, and working out exactly where to push the boundaries, is important. It is usually less risky in times of uncertainty to try things out and occasionally fail than to play safe and get stuck.

Personal development can be an uncomfortable process, and many people struggle with that. We have to be brave enough to experiment with different ways of behaving, not all of which will succeed. Children do this all the time and learn from their mistakes. That can be much harder as adults when we feel we have more to lose, or are (perhaps realistically) concerned about the impact on our own image and reputation of making mistakes. This is why older people can sometimes be reluctant to put themselves on the line and learn new skills. They do not want to be embarrassed. Yet this can be self-limiting. Research on neuroplasticity shows we are able to continue to learn throughout our lives. A positive attitude makes many things possible and a sense of humour helps keep everything in perspective.

Along with courage, we need to develop the confidence, perseverance, patience and resilience to keep going and recover from the inevitable setbacks we encounter. Keeping physically fit, making sure we get enough rest, and looking after ourselves properly are all important. We can also look at ways of developing our mental toughness, which some people manage to accomplish quite quickly.

Managing relationships

Uncertain situations place a strain on relationships because they continually test the strength of trust. Not only do we need allies in times of uncertainty to provide emotional support and get things done, but we have to build relationships with people we might not agree with, like or even trust if we are to make the most of things. A proactive approach requires us to get on with a wide variety of people, encouraging a diversity of views, robust challenge, debate and dialogue to find the best way forward. This rarely comes only from those who are similar to us. And once the best course of action is clear, we usually need support from a surprisingly wide variety of people to put it into practice.

Building relationships is a long-term process, with the strength of the relationships being tested at every interaction. Whether we trust someone depends partly on their credibility – whether they are sincere, reliable, and have a good reputation. As time passes, we begin to make our own assessments of their competence and effectiveness. Longer term, we maintain relationships with people either because we feel obliged to for moral reasons; we decide to for rational or contractual reasons, or because we want to remain connected, having developed an emotional attachment based on familiarity, friendship or personal confidence.

Building trust at this deep level makes it easier to deal with uncertainty. People will stick with us even through difficult times. How can we achieve this?

• Use empathy and emotional intelligence.

• Make an effort to get to know, understand and connect with people as individuals, rather than simply as professionals, associates or clients.

• It is not just a question of getting to know people personally but really being able to see and feel things from their perspective.

• Ask what matters to them rather than what is the matter with them.

Having respect for people is essential. In the course of our work, we developed a good rapport with Jim Cherry, the former President and CEO of Aéroports de Montréal, and talked to him about this topic. Jim, who retired in 2016 after a highly successful career, told us that, before making a final decision on recruiting someone for his senior team, he took them to dinner at a local restaurant. He was not checking their table manners, conversation skills or knowledge of fine cuisine. Rather, he was taking note of how they treated the waiter. Did they treat the waiter with respect? He only hired those who did.

There are additional practical points worth considering:

• Act consistently, starting with small steps and building on them.

• Gain a reputation for delivering what we promise.

• When we do have to negotiate, it is best to do that in a principled way that maintains the quality of relationships.

• And if relationships are to be sustainable, reciprocity is crucial. It's almost impossible to build a strong relationship with someone who only takes and never gives.

Building our character and core

It is our character and sense of purpose which bring together all the competencies discussed above to keep us well-grounded, not afraid to be authentic and true to what we believe. When dealing with an uncertain environment, it is helpful to have certainty in ourselves.

While our personalities may be relatively stable over time, we can work to develop our own character if we are prepared to reflect on what we are doing, challenge the clarity and relevance of our own sense of purpose and values, and keep our approach to ethical issues under review.

Even when we pay attention to these steps, developing ourselves takes time. Although we may be convinced intellectually that we should take action, it can take a long time before 'the switch goes on' and we actually decide to do something about it. Often it takes a crisis or some kind of emotional awakening, a realisation that our behaviour is having an impact on ourselves or others, to encourage us to try different ways of behaving. If these are successful, we develop new habits and ways of conducting ourselves, which are eventually reflected in our deeper character.

• The most effective way to develop personal leadership is through a combination of experience, formal training, mentoring and coaching.

• Building strengths through exposure to progressively challenging situations interspersed with periods of more formal development is another way of doing this.

• It helps to have had previous experience of tough and uncertain times and to have come through them successfully.

• Building a sense of core purpose comes from within and cannot be forced on somebody from the outside.

• We need to be psychologically ready to change. It requires a conscious decision to act, as well as a preparedness to take the necessary steps.

• Effort and persistence bring reward.

In the final analysis, personal leadership skills develop when the conditions are right. The problem is that currently these skills are not being systematically encouraged in our societies in a way that makes them the norm rather than the exception. In the next chapter, we will explore how this might be achieved.

CHAPTER 11

Implications for Organisations and Society

'Don't blame the mouse, blame the hole in the wall.'

The Talmud

Challenging change

To what extent do our societies, institutions and organisations support, encourage and educate people to take a proactive approach to uncertainty? To what extent do our leaders act as role models and ambassadors for the values that underpin this, such as responsibility, courage, positivity, respect, empathy, compassion, curiosity, freedom and truth? To what extent are people enthusiastically grasping the opportunities inherent in an uncertain world?

Unfortunately, 'not very much' is the answer to all of these questions. A large number of people seem to be on the defensive, choosing to close themselves off, disregarding facts which don't suit them, reverting to conventional ways, blaming society for their ills, and looking for someone else to sort things out. And that 'someone else' is all too often a populist leader with scant regard for the truth, spreading fake news. There is an apparent backlash against tolerance and openness.

Why is this? To understand what is happening, let us take a step back. As we discussed earlier, we are living in a period of global transition. We are leaving behind a world of relative stability and entering one where our social, political, environmental and economic systems are in a state of flux. New technologies, in particular artificial intelligence, have the potential to change our lives in ways we cannot yet imagine.

On the positive side of the ledger, there is strong evidence that our lives continue to improve. In his book *Factfulness*, the late Swedish physician and academic Hans Rosling argues that by most objective measures, 'things are better than [we] think'. He points out that there have been amazing improvements in all countries over the last 200 years. We are living much longer, are in better health, have less poverty and have far more choice – as consumers, in lifestyle, in how we live our lives. Yet sometimes it seems that the better off we are, the worse we feel.

• We are witnessing ever-increasing self-medication, higher levels of reported anxiety among young people, and record numbers diagnosed with obesity and diabetes.

• Rates of depression have increased markedly over the last fifty years in many countries. The American psychologist Professor Martin Seligman notes that in the USA the rate has risen from around 1–2 per cent for those born in the 1920s to over 20 per cent for those born more recently.

• Depression has become a common medical diagnosis, ranking just behind back pain.

Unpredictability, uncertainty, and the rapid pace of change seem to lie behind this. The institutions and systems that were developed in the past – financial, educational, political, faith – struggle to adapt and remain relevant to what is happening today. Our blind trust in authority and institutions has diminished over the past three decades or so as we have become better educated and informed. Our communities have become more fragmented, and it can be harder to find support when things go wrong. Our expectations are also higher: we are linked through social media to many 'contacts' we barely know personally whose public images suggest that they are doing better than us, while other online platforms, as well as the traditional media, allow us to compare ourselves at any time against the most gifted and talented in the world. It is no wonder we can feel as if we are losing out.

In addition to these challenges, people have understandable fears and concerns about what might be in store for them in the future, collectively and individually. There are no certain answers. Questions come from all sides of the political landscape.

• What impact will new technology and artificial intelligence have?

• Will there be a need for my skills?

• How will I earn a living?

• What will my local community be like in the future?

• What are the risks of terrorism or global conflict?

• Are we doing enough about the environment?

• What kind of world will it be for my children and grandchildren?

So perhaps it is not surprising that, despite all the apparent signs that we are living in a golden age of unparalleled freedom and prosperity, many people feel that things are falling apart and that they and their societies are under threat. There is always a substantial minority of the population which leans towards authoritarianism – a desire for security, order, power and status and a preference for structured lines of authority, conventional values and obedience. When societies feel under threat this proportion increases and authoritarian views become increasingly influential.

In these circumstances, people tend to favour cultures that are 'tight', with strong social norms, strict rules, little tolerance for deviance, and strong, autocratic leaders prepared to enforce the norms. Such cultures are unlikely to welcome newcomers or be tolerant of different behaviours. However, they seem to be attractive to some people. They generally have higher levels of social order, with lower rates of crime and fewer problems of self-regulation such as obesity, debt or drug addiction. They provide people with a degree of certainty and structure.

Unfortunately, as tight cultures are not open, tolerant, creative or flexible, they are ill-suited to exploring new ideas or taking advantage of the opportunities arising from uncertainty. Social cohesion counts for more than innovation. Caution is more important than adventure. Whether led by populist leaders on the right, or inspired by the certain ideological conviction of those on the left, a 'tight' culture is not an environment which encourages the proactive approach to uncertainty we have been advocating. The cost of certainty is too high when power and control count for more than collaboration and truth.

Institutional barriers

Our institutions and systems can also be barriers to change. Take the education system, for example, which has its roots in the industrial era and teaching young people to learn and repeat information correctly from a defined curriculum. Traditionally, this has been delivered through schools and by structured, individual, teacher-led classroom-based learning. The system was designed in a period when children had limited access to information. With a focus on exams it can seem as if there is a greater emphasis on learning facts than on encouraging creativity. While in former times what was learned was designed to last a lifetime and there were institutional barriers to re-skilling and re-educating the adult population, there is growing awareness of the need to address this deficit.

In a different sector, consider the weight we attach to regulations and detailed procedures as a way of exercising central control. The financial sector provides an example. Rules, procedures and regulation are seen as the principal vehicles for changing behaviour; weaknesses are found, detailed laws drafted, and the resources of the authorities focused on finding transgressors, prosecuting and punishing them. This can lead to people becoming overly cautious or focusing their energy on loopholes in the rules, rather than encouraging the fundamental changes in attitude and mindset required.

In addition, these are still bureaucratic institutions that focus on hierarchy, top-down control, micro-management, 'doing what you are told', and rigidly defined procedures. In the worse cases this can lead to dictatorial and bullying management, with insufficient attention paid to people and innovation. These are environments where it can be a challenge to get a proactive approach off the ground.

Finally, those in power can be reluctant to share information. Power and truth are not always natural bedfellows. Giving comprehensive data to those lower down the pecking order can be seen as risky. There is a possibility of losing control; too much challenge can result in delays and procrastination; and too many ideas can lead to confusion.

It is superficially easier for those in power if people are discouraged from acting too independently and therefore do not challenge them too much.

The systemic barriers to developing more people with the personal leadership skills to take control and shape their immediate environment in ways that take advantage of uncertainty are therefore substantial. Such obstacles are centred around fear, in the broadest sense of what this might mean for our societies; institutionalised and strongly rooted attitudes, behaviours and practices that focus on maintaining centralised control; and at a personal level, for those in power, a desire to stay in power and maintain the status quo.

Powerful enablers

While some may wish to maintain the status quo, the forces for change have never been stronger. Increasing longevity, the '100 year life', makes adapting to change a necessity. Advances in technology, particularly artificial intelligence, are forcing people to reinvent themselves if they want to feel that they are useful members of society. People have to learn new skills throughout their lives and may have to change organisations and jobs more frequently. They are likely to have to be more entrepreneurial and less dependent on a long-term employer for their social status and financial security.

People are already concerned about the impact of a changing world on their psychological well-being and are demanding a better life. Generally speaking, people feel happier, more fulfilled, and operate at a higher level when they are more in control of their environment. Once people begin to feel helpless, their health can suffer. This is a strong reason in its own right for building people's capacity to cope.

More generally, competitive pressures put an intense focus on the performance shortcomings of organisations that adopt an overly defensive approach. At its most basic level, this can be attributed to the costs of supervision and control. Flatter structures and a higher degree of self-management are inherently less expensive than traditional hierarchical structures and provide more motivation. We have worked with many organisations over the years, from oil refineries to providers of health and social care, which operate in this way. Buurtzorg, the Dutch nurse-led model of community care, is an excellent example of how effective a collaborative, client-centred approach can be in practice.

A defensive approach, on the other hand, is associated with the inability to respond rapidly to changing circumstances, and a lack of innovation. Defensiveness on its own is no longer a viable strategy for cutting-edge, high-performance organisations. For example, in the highly competitive world of professional sport, the performance edge is increasingly found in individuals and teams that take a positive, proactive approach. Innovative ideas and tactics quickly become the norm. Topspin backhands in tennis, the 'reverse sweep' in cricket, and the 'bend it like Beckham' swerving free kick in soccer – all once rare and only seen at elite levels – are now commonplace.

Larger numbers of proactive people can enable organisations and societies to operate successfully in smaller units and at a more local level. A desire for greater autonomy and control lies at the heart of the political move away from a multinational and international focus to a more localised agenda. Why should it stop there?

We know that IT systems are increasingly capable of supporting distributed leadership through linking people, teams and the broader environment. If we also have more people with the personal leadership qualities needed to take responsibility, manage risk and think for themselves, it becomes much easier to create connected organisations of small, agile, autonomous, accountable teams rather than large monolithic bureaucracies. The benefits of scale for investment, purchasing, and strategic leverage can be combined with the agility and entrepreneurial ethos of smaller teams.

These kinds of organisations already exist, and when they work well are flexible, customer-focused, and have a strong capacity for learning. They provide a more human scale, a sense of identity and collegiality, a more sustainable approach, a better environment for enhancing well-being, and a massive opportunity for improved organisation effectiveness.

The way ahead

What can be done to move things forward? If we are serious about preparing people for an uncertain world, we need a change of mindset at senior levels in society and a reorientation of our institutions.

The focus of our society, institutions and organisations should be on helping to create environments that encourage people to take responsibility and act proactively, rather than on enforcing centralised control.

Start at the beginning, with education. If uncertainty is so important, it would be sensible to ensure that from an early age our children are given the tools to deal with it. Education systems vary greatly, but a formal focus on the three 'Rs' – reading, writing and arithmetic – is insufficient. Today's learners also need four 'Cs' – skills in critical thinking, creativity, collaboration and communication – to deal successfully with the challenges of uncertainty and change they seem bound to face. They will also need to develop personal qualities: taking responsibility, being proactive, taking risks, being resilient, and displaying empathy and compassion.

Some of these skills can be taught in the conventional way, but experiential learning and project assignments need to be a larger part of the mix. Developing character, confidence and resilience is something that good schools have always done, with the development of social responsibility and compassion among the more recent themes. It is a question of finding ways to extend this 'best practice' more widely – and making it more readily available for people at all life stages.

Giving people responsibility at an early stage is particularly helpful. Providing them with opportunities to undertake challenging projects where there is not a simple black-and-white answer, where they are encouraged to think for themselves, and where they need to work with and interact with others and not just on their own, is also valuable. And there is no doubt that extra-mural activities, such as sport, getting involved in community organisations, playing music, part-time work, and travel, can make a tremendous difference to individuals' personal development and may well turn out to be more important to them than what they remember from the academic curriculum.

LEARNING TO THINK FOR YOURSELF
(Terri)

Sister Simone, our science teacher, was adamant that girls should get a thorough grounding in scientific methodology and maths. She introduced me to the Fibonacci numbers and suggested that I do a 'project' on them. This opened up the world of the golden mean, ratios, sequences and applied scientific formulae. Hours were spent in the library searching for references. My project utilised paper, poster board, photographs of architectural buildings, and pieces of twigs and shells to illustrate my findings. My interest in Mathematics was awakened.

Focus more on principles and less on regulation. Of course, there are times when regulations are worthwhile, but if we fall into the trap of thinking that obeying detailed procedures and enforcing legislation are the only ways of influencing and controlling behaviour, we can too often end up with a tangle of bureaucratic rules and regulations that are neither necessary nor effective. In a complex and changing world, they may even be inappropriate. If regulations are over-complicated, people may not bother to read them, let alone try to understand the intention behind them.

If the potential punishments are too severe, either substantial energy is expended on getting around the rules, or initiative and independent thinking are stifled.

What starts off as sensible in theory becomes counter-productive in practice.

We now know that punitive legislation is not the only way to shape or influence behaviours, and is not even the most effective. Instead, our default position should be to find ways of getting people to take responsibility for themselves. Very often it makes sense to invest time and effort upfront in communication, explanation and dialogue so that people understand the underlying reasons for change. More systematic training can help with the details.

There are other ways of achieving results if dialogue and training aren't enough. In their influential book *Nudge*, authors Thaler and Sunstein describe how 'choice architectures' can be set up to nudge people in the desired direction. Policies and systems can be designed to make preferred behaviours easier and more natural than others, and incentives provided to encourage or discourage different courses of action. Communications can be framed in ways that make desirable actions more likely. Simple changes to the phrasing of a letter accompanying a tax demand, for example, can result in higher compliance. Provided there is transparency around principles, there is no inherent ethical issue to adopting these approaches as an alternative to legislation.

Educate organisation leaders. Unfortunately, there are too many people in senior positions who only know how to operate in an autocratic 'command and control' manner and who lack the skills to lead, inspire, engage and develop the people who work for them. Not only does this result in suboptimal organisation performance, it ruins many people's lives and prevents them from fulfilling their potential. Attempting to impose order in a genuinely complex system is a futile undertaking – far better to stand back a little, make sure everyone understands what is expected of them, and provide support. In organisations where innovation is needed, this is critical. Andy Grove, the legendary ex-CEO of Intel, summed this up when he talked about 'letting chaos reign' – avoiding micromanagement and allowing innovative and creative ideas to emerge – which then needs to be followed by 'reining in chaos', where judgement is needed to ensure things do not get out of control.

Create the space to listen and reflect. Our capacity to cope with uncertainty is limited by the demands of our everyday lives. Too often, we are so busy getting on with things that we don't have time to listen properly to others and think through how things are changing. Our institutions need to ensure that they invest sufficient time in listening to people, researching and exploring possible futures, and preparing for different eventualities. Our organisations need to structure their agendas so that a proportion of time is spent on strategic thinking as well as on operations. And as individuals we need to ensure that we are not so overloaded that we lose our ability to see things in perspective.

We need to mind ourselves and others.

'Now that we have written this book, what are your views on uncertainty?' asked Richard.

'I'm really not sure,' Terri replied.

GLOSSARY

360-degree feedback
An organisational process where an individual gets structured feedback from colleagues at all levels that can be used to gain insights into how (s)he is perceived

Accepting strategy
This involves accepting that much of what happens is outside our control and focuses on controlling our own reactions and responses while continuing to scan the environment

ACT
Acceptance commitment therapy encourages people to accept what is out of their control and commit to actions that improve their life

Attention deficit trait
A dysfunctional pattern of behaviour where people become so overwhelmed with information and data they are unable to focus properly on anything

Authoritarian personality
A desire for security, order, power and status with structured lines of authority

CBT
Cognitive behavioural therapy looks at how thoughts, beliefs and attitudes affect feelings and behaviours

Chaotic system
In a chaotic system, only turbulence exists and there is no relationship between cause and effect. It is impossible to predict the future behaviour of any complex chaotic system

Complex system
Complex systems are characterised by unpredictability, flux, change. The relationship between cause and effect only becomes clear in retrospect

Complicated system
In a complicated system, there is often more than one right answer and, while there is a relationship between cause and effect, it is not obvious to everyone

Confirmation bias
Looking for data to support preconceived ideas

Cynefin framework
A conceptual framework used to guide decision-making and leadership behaviours based on systems thinking

Defensive mindset
A default mindset for dealing with uncertainty which involves protecting ourselves psychologically by minimising or rejecting new information and adopting familiar patterns of behaviour

Disrupting strategy
A strategy which involves challenging the status quo and underlying assumptions. Responsible disruption means doing this in an ethical way consistent with a broader vision

Exploring strategy
A strategy which involves trying to develop a clearer understanding of a situation so we are in a better position to both control and take advantage of opportunities

Flynn effect
The consistent rise in IQ test scores observed in young people over the last fifty years

Groupthink
The practice of thinking as a group; discounting information from external sources if it does not fit the group's firmly held view; sticking rigidly to a viewpoint as a group although the evidence points to a different reality

Imposing strategy
A strategy which involves attempting to impose our own view of the world and what the future should look like

Loss aversion
Giving undue weight to preserving what we have

Maginot Line
A line of concrete fortifications, obstacles and weapons installations built by France in the 1930s to deter invasion by Germany

Mindfulness
A mental state achieved by focusing one's awareness on the present moment, while calmly acknowledging and accepting one's feelings, thoughts, and bodily sensations

Neuroplasticity
The lifelong capacity of the brain to change and rewire itself in response to the stimulation of learning and experience

Nudge theory
This explains how changes in the environment can influence people to behave in particular ways

Optimism bias
A tendency to underestimate the downside of any chosen course of action – also known as unrealistic optimism or comparative optimism

PDCA cycle
An approach to quality management advocated by Deming – Plan, Do, Check, Act

PESTEL analysis
An analysis of a situation looked at from Political, Economic, Social, Technological, Environmental and Legislative perspectives

Proactive mindset
A flexible, pragmatic, outward-looking approach for dealing with uncertainty based on the Richmor Model

Psychometric tests
Used to objectively measure individual characteristics such as cognitive abilities, personality, behavioural style and attitudes

Reframing
Looking at things from a different perspective or through a different mental model than we have used in the past

Richmor Competencies
The attitudes, skills and behaviours ideally needed to deal with uncertainty

Richmor Cycle
An approach to dealing with uncertainty that can be used on an ongoing basis

Richmor Framework
A generic framework which includes all elements of the Richmor approach for dealing with uncertainty

Richmor Model
A conceptual model used to guide actions in uncertain times

Richmor Plains
This refers to relatively stable periods of time with low levels of uncertainty

Richmor Range
This refers to periods of time where there is a great deal of uncertainty, complexity, volatility and ambiguity

Richmor Ridge
This refers to a specific episode, event or period of time characterised by a great deal of uncertainty

Richmor Steps
This describes the four-stage approach to dealing with uncertainty used in the Richmor Model

Richmor Strategies
This is a set of five psychological strategies for dealing with uncertainty

Safe to fail trial
An approach to experimentation which ensures that the consequences of failure are thought through and managed in advance

Scenario planning
A structured approach to strategic planning which tests plans against a number of possible future environments

Self-confidence bias
We tend to believe our judgement and abilities are better than they are

Shamrock Model
A model of the Richmor Competencies which includes personal, interpersonal and conceptual components

Simple system
Simple systems are characterised by stability, and clear, direct relationships between cause and effect that are apparent to everyone

STOPP
A technique designed to help people who are feeling anxious or concerned to regain control of their emotions (Stop; Take a breath; Observe; Pull back; Proceed)

Sunk costs
Favouring something we have already invested in

SWOT analysis
An analysis of a situation looking at Strengths, Weaknesses, Opportunities and Threats

Tight culture
A culture with strong social norms, strict rules, little tolerance for deviance and strong autocratic leaders

Trial and success
A strategy intended to encourage a positive approach to experimentation which builds rapidly on successful trials and discards failures

Type 1 & Type 2 thinking
Type 1 thinking is fast, instinctive and emotional, whereas Type 2 is slower, considered and thoughtful (Kahneman)

Uncertainty avoidance
The degree of tolerance a society displays towards uncertain and ambiguous situations (Hofstede)

Vertical development
Advancements in a person's thinking that enable them to think in more complex, strategic, systemic and interdependent ways. This contrasts with horizontal development, which is about the acquisition of specific skills and knowledge

VUCA world
A world characterised by **V**olatility, **U**ncertainty, **C**omplexity and **A**mbiguity

OTHER RESOURCES

American Psychological Association: **www.apa.org**
(Professional association for US psychologists)

Association for Business Psychology: **www.theabp.org.uk**
(Professional association for business psychologists)

Australian Psychological Society: **www.psychology.org.au**
(Professional representative body for psychologists in Australia)

Aware: **www.aware.ie**
(Support and information on anxiety and depression)

British Psychological Society: **www.bps.org.uk**
(A representative body for psychologists and psychology in the
United Kingdom)

Canadian Psychological Association: **www.cpa.ca**
(The primary organisation representing psychologists throughout
Canada)

Chambers Ireland: **www.chambers.ie**
(Coordinating body which facilitates networking and growth of
Ireland's chambers of commerce)

Cognitive Behavioural Psychotherapy Ireland: **www.cbti.ie**
(Accreditation body for cognitive behavioural psychotherapy in
Ireland)

Enterprise Ireland: **www.enterprise-ireland.com**
(Irish government agency responsible for developing Irish
enterprise in world markets)

European Federation of Psychologists' Associations: **www.efpa.eu**
(Umbrella organisation for European psychological associations)

Family Therapy Association of Ireland:
www.familytherapyireland.com
(Information on therapy for individuals, couples and families)

Health Service Executive: **www.hse.ie/eng/services/list**
(The HSE provides health and social services in hospitals, health
facilities and in communities across Ireland)

Institute of Directors: **www.iod.com**
(Business organisation for company directors and senior managers
in the UK)

Irish Association for Counselling and Psychotherapy: **www.iacp.ie**
(Professional association for counsellors and psychotherapists)

Irish Business and Employers Confederation: **www.ibec.ie**
(Ireland's largest and most influential business organisation for
information on policy and business supports)

Irish Council for Psychotherapy: **www.psychotherapycouncil.ie**
(Information on psychotherapy services in Ireland)

Local Enterprise Offices: **www.localenterprise.ie**
(Information and support on starting or growing a business in
Ireland, including a women's network for women entrepreneurs)

Mental Health Ireland: **www.mentalhealthireland.ie**
(Promotion of positive mental health and well-being in Ireland)

National Health Service: **www.nhs.uk**
(Publicly funded UK health service – supports include CBT and other forms of talking therapies for anxiety and stress)

Psychological Society of Ireland: **www.psychologicalsociety.ie**
(Professional body for psychologists and psychology in the Republic of Ireland)

Samaritans: **www.samaritans.org/ireland**
(Confidential 24-hour support service for people who are depressed, suicidal or in need)

St Patrick's Mental Health Services: **www.stpatricks.ie**
(Mental health services including community, outpatient care, day patient services and inpatient care)

UK Council for Psychotherapy: **www.psychotherapy.org.uk**
(Organisation for the accreditation and regulation of UK counsellors and psychotherapists)

OTHER READING

This book brings together our personal experiences, as well as incorporating research, knowledge and examples from a variety of sources.

We have found two recent books interesting, given that we have adopted this way of working: Brian Hughes' logical account of the methodological issues associated with scientific psychology, *Psychology in Crisis*, and Adina Tarry's robust advocacy for learning from practice in her *Coaching with Careers and AI in Mind*.

While we were writing our book, Jordan Peterson's *12 Rules for Life* was published, in which the author draws on his academic and clinical psychology experience to provide a set of rules which are intended to reduce uncertainty and provide a structured order to people's lives. In our book, we start from the premise that uncertainty is inevitable and that the real challenge is to learn not just how to cope with it, but how to deal with it head on and make the most of the opportunities it offers.

Ackroyd, P., *History of England, Vol. 5* (London: Macmillan, 2018)

Adams, D., *The Hitchhiker's Guide to the Galaxy* (New York: Macmillan, 2009)

Baines, G., *Meaning Inc: The blueprint for business success in the 21st century* (London: Profile Books, 2007)

Bennett, N. and Lemoine, G., 'What VUCA Really Means for You', *Harvard Business Review*, vol. 92, nos. 1–2, 2014

Briers, S., *Brilliant Cognitive Behavioural Therapy* (New York: Pearson Prentice-Hall, 2009)

Bruch, H. and Ghoshal, S., 'Beware the Busy Manager', *Harvard Business Review*, March 2002

Cialdini, R.B., *Influence: The psychology of persuasion* (New York: HarperCollins, 2007)

Covey, Stephen R., *The 7 Habits of Highly Effective People* (New York: Simon & Schuster, 1989)

Duhigg, C., *The Power of Habit* (New York: Random House, 2013)

Flynn, J.R., *Are We Getting Smarter? Rising IQ in the twenty-first century* (Cambridge: Cambridge University Press, 2012)

Gelfand, M., *Rule Makers, Rule Breakers: How tight and loose cultures wire our world* (New York: Simon & Schuster, 2018)

Goleman, D., *Emotional Intelligence: Why it can matter more than IQ* (London: Bloomsbury, 1996)

Goodhart, D., *The Road to Somewhere* (London: Hurst & Co., 2017)

Gratton, L. and Scott, A., *The 100-Year Life* (London: Bloomsbury, 2017)

Gray, D., *The Connected Company* (San Francisco: O'Reilly, 2012)

Hallowell, E.M. and Ratey, J.J., *Driven to Distraction* (New York: Penguin Random House, 2011)

Hansen, M.T., *Great at Work* (New York: Simon & Schuster, 2018)

Harari, Y.N., *21 Lessons for the 21st Century* (London: Jonathan Cape, 2018)

Hastings, M., 'We're in a Dark Age Where Hearts Rule Minds', *The Sunday Times*, 13 October 2018; https://www.thetimes.co.uk/article/we-re-in-a-dark-age-where-hearts-rule-minds-5p7gl6g5q [accessed 17 November 2019]

Hofstede, G., *Culture's Consequences: International differences in work-related values* (Thousand Oaks, CA: Sage Publications, 1984)

Hughes, B., *Psychology in Crisis* (New York: Macmillan International, 2018)

Kahane, A., *Collaborating with the Enemy* (San Francisco: Berrett-Koehler Publishers, 2017)

Kahneman, D., *Thinking: Fast and slow* (New York: Penguin, 2012)

Kotter, J.P., *A Sense of Urgency* (Brighton, MA: Harvard Business Review Press, 2008)

Laloux, F., *Reinventing Organizations* (New York: Nelson Parker, 2014)

Lewis, M., *The Undoing Project* (New York: Penguin, 2017)

Manns, M.L. and Rising, L., *More Fearless Change: Strategies for making your ideas happen* (Boston: Addison-Wesley, 2015)

Marshall, T., *Divided: Why we are living in an age of walls* (London: Elliott & Thompson, 2018)

Meyer, E., *The Culture Map* (New York: International Edition PublicAffairs, 2015)

Morrell, M. and Capparrell, S., *Shackleton's Way: Leadership lessons of the great Antarctic explorer* (New York: Deckle Edge, 2002)

National Education Association, *Preparing 21st Century Students for a Global Society: An educator's guide to the 'Four Cs'* (2012); https://www.academia.edu/36311252/Preparing_21st_Century_Students_for_a_Global_Society_An_Educators_Guide_to_the_Four_Cs_Great_Public_Schools_for_Every_Student [accessed 17 November 2019]

Peterson, J.B., *12 Rules for Life: An antidote to chaos* (London: Penguin Random House, 2018)

Petrie, N., 'Vertical Leadership Development – Part 1: Developing leaders for a complex world' (white paper, 2015); https://www.ccl.org/wp-content/uploads/2015/04/VerticalLeadersPart1.pdf [accessed 17 November 2019]

Pinker, S., *Enlightenment Now* (New York: Penguin Random House, 2018)

Plenty, R. and Morrissey, T., 'Courageous Leadership: Lessons from Nelson Mandela', *Airport World*, June–July 2014, p. 53

Plenty, R. and Morrissey, T., 'More Than Just Results', *Airport World*, June–July 2013, pp. 62–4

Plenty, R. and Morrissey, T., 'Motivating and Retaining Employees', in E. Curtis and J. Cullen (eds), *Leadership and Change for the Health Professional* (London: Open University Press, 2017)

Prochaska, J.O., DiClemente, C.C. and Norcross, J., 'In Search of How People Change', *American Psychologist*, vol. 47, 1992, pp. 1102–14

Rock, D., 'SCARF: A brain-based model for collaborating and influencing others', *NeuroLeadership Journal*, vol. 1, 2008, pp. 1–9

Rosling, H., *Factfulness* (London: Sceptre, 2018)

Rowland, D., *Still Moving: How to lead mindful change* (London: Wiley Blackwell, 2017)

Seligman, M., *Learned Optimism: How to change your mind and your life* (New York: Vintage Books, 2006 [1990])

Senge, P.M., *The Fifth Discipline: The art and practice of the learning organization*, 2nd revised edn (New York: Random House Business, 2006)

Sharot, T., *The Optimism Bias* (London: Robinson Publishing, 2012)

Snowden, D.J. and Boone, M.E., 'A Leader's Framework for Decision-Making', *Harvard Business Review*, November 2007, pp. 1–10

Strycharczyk, D. and Clough, P., *Developing Mental Toughness: Coaching strategies to improve performance, resilience and well-being*, 2nd edn (London: Kogan Page, 2015)

Tarry, A., 'Valuing Experience and the Power of Past Practice', in *Coaching with Careers and AI in Mind* (London: Routledge, 2018)

Thaler, R.H. and Sunstein, C.R., *Nudge* (New York: Penguin Books, 2009)

The King's Fund, *Leadership and Engagement for Improvement in the NHS: Together we can* (London: The King's Fund, 2012)

Trompenaars, F. and Hampden-Turner, C., *Riding the Waves of Culture*, 3rd edn (Boston: Nicholas Brealey, 2012)

INDEX